AF600047

THE CATHOLIC UNIVERSITY OF AMERICA
CANON LAW STUDIES
No. 350

THE SECRET ARCHIVES OF THE DIOCESAN CURIA

A Historical Synopsis and a Commentary

A DISSERTATION

SUBMITTED TO THE FACULTY OF THE SCHOOL OF CANON LAW OF THE CATHOLIC UNIVERSITY OF AMERICA IN PARTIAL FULFILLMENT OF THE REQUIREMENTS FOR THE DEGREE OF DOCTOR OF CANON LAW

BY THE
REVEREND CHARLES A. KEKUMANO, A.B., J.C.L.
PRIEST OF THE DIOCESE OF HONOLULU

THE CATHOLIC UNIVERSITY OF AMERICA PRESS
WASHINGTON, D. C.
1954

NIHIL OBSTAT:
Clemens V. Bastnagel, J.U.D.
Censor Deputatus
Washingtonii, D. C., die 5 aprilis, 1954

IMPRIMATUR
✠ Jacobus J. Sweeney, D.D.
Episcopus Honoluluensis
Sancti Francisci, die 7 aprilis, 1954

MANUFACTURED BY
UNIVERSAL LITHOGRAPHERS, INC.
BALTIMORE, MD., U. S. A.

Respectfully Dedicated

with

Reverence and Gratitude

to

His Excellency

The Most Rev. James J. Sweeney, D.D.,

Bishop of Honolulu

TABLE OF CONTENTS

FOREWORD

The preservation of important records has long been recognized as an essential factor in good administration. It is hardly necessary to note that history has become largely dependent on archives.

The ancient civilizations of Israel, Phoenicia, Egypt, Greece and Rome appreciated the value of preserving important documents, and usually reserved for the archives a part of the temple. The sacredness of the holy place was expected to be an additional guarantee against violation. Thus, documents were to be carefully preserved for official reference.

The early Church of Rome inherited this reverence and respect for records and set up primitive safes for the proper custody of the sacred vessels and the Holy Scriptures. The home of some worthy Christian family served as a depository at first, and then later, during the persecutions, some secret chamber in the catacombs was used.

In the historical section of this study it is not intended to give an exhaustive enumeration of the references to archives from the earliest times to the present. This would not be practical, nor would it be necessary, for gaining a general view of the historical development of archives, and especially of the secret archives. Instead, the aim is to trace the legal history of diocesan archives and to indicate the natural growth of a separate depository for the documents of a more secret character.

Generally, legislation indicates the directing, administrative hand of authority making provision for the needs of the community. Historically, then, legislation serves as an index of the prevalent *modus agendi.* Since there is no specific legislation on archives in general, or on secret archives in particular, during the first sixteen centuries, the historical section of this dissertation is necessarily brief. Nevertheless it is important to note the constant indications from earliest times of an archival system of some kind. Furthermore, the historical references show the solicitude and diligence of the Church to protect and preserve the important letters, records and documents of the perfectly self-contained society instituted by Christ.

The second part of the work is a canonical commentary on the present law of the Church regarding the diocesan secret archives. Throughout the canonical discussion the responsibility of the residential bishop is stressed. The secret archives of the diocese can be important in the administration of the diocese, and the canons here considered succinctly outline the general principles that serve to guide the residential bishop in his handling of confidential or highly secret documents.

Most of the canonical commentaries offer only a brief treatment on the diocesan secret archives. Therefore it has been found necessary to assemble the individual points from these commentaries and to analyze them in respect to the purpose of the secret archives as established in the Code. Particularly in the chapter on the contents of the secret archives, it was necessary to consider the indications given in the Code itself as also additional materials that naturally suggest exceptional custody and preservation.

The writer has sought to present a practical explanation of a misunderstood and perhaps ignored canonical institute. The secret archives of the diocese are not simply an interesting phenomenon that reflects the responsibility for the keeping of two keys, or the collection either of the foibles of the clergy or of accusations made against some of their members. The secret archives are the legal depository for those documents and writings which, by their nature or by determination in law, demand secrecy in their custody and use.

The writer welcomes this occasion to acknowledge his sincere gratitude to His Excellency, the Most Reverend James J. Sweeney, D. D., Bishop of Honolulu, for the opportunity of advanced study in Canon Law at the Catholic University of America. The writer also wishes to thank the members of the Faculty of the School of Canon Law, his classmates at the University, and all others whose scholarly guidance, helpful suggestions, and kind encouragement have made this dissertation possible.

CHAPTER I

LEGISLATION PRIOR TO THE COUNCIL OF TRENT

Article I. First Centuries up to Justinian

There was very little written ecclesiastical law in the first three centuries of the Church's existence. Divine and apostolic traditions as well as custom guided the faithful of these early times. Furthermore, the successive waves of persecution that battered the Church as well as the extreme difficulties of communication made it impossible for the Church to have any universally precise systematic legislation.[1]

It is a matter of record, of course, that the Apostles and their immediate successors did lay down regulations and precepts as problems arose.[2] But actually, up to the fourth century the Church was necessarily cautious and discreet in legislative activity. The fact that there is no legislation in these first centuries regarding either archives in general or secret archives in particular is therefore readily understood. No specific occasion seems to have arisen demanding such action. And yet occasional historical references seem to imply the existence of ecclesiastical archives from the earliest years. And in the course of time the historical references occasionally suggest such delicate matters which would require the use of safeguards now afforded by secret archives.

The *Liber Pontificalis* claims that Pope St. Clement (ca. 88-97) divided the Church at Rome into seven regions, and assigned to these regions notaries who were to compile accurate and diligent accounts of the acts of the martyrs.[3] No explanation was given concerning the method or place of preservation of these records. Most likely this administrative action was patterned on a procedure similar to that of the civil government. Regardless of whether

---

[1] Kurtscheid, *Historia Iuris Canonici, Historia Institutorum,* Vol. I (ab Ecclesiae fundatione usque ad Gratianum), (Romae: Officium Libri Catholici, 1941). pp. 1-96.

[2] Acts of the Apostles, VI: 3; XI; XV.

[3] "Hic (Clemens) fecit VII regiones, dividit notariis fidelibus ecclesiae, qui gestas martyrum sollicite et curiose unusquisque per regionem suam, diligenter perquireret."—Duchesne, *Le Liber Pontificalis* (2 vols., 1886-1892), I, 123 (hereafter cited as *Liber Pontificalis*).

these were true notaries in the sense of later legislation, this early reference to a definite group with the specific task of recording historical deeds indicates the concern of even the apostolic era for the preservation of important records.

The *Liber Pontificalis,* speaking later of the same notaries in the reign of Pope Anteros (235-236) asserts: "Hic (Anteros) gesta martyrum diligenter a notariis exquisivit et in ecclesia recondit . . ."[4] And here the reference to an ecclesiastical archive is the clearest up to this date. The words *"in ecclesia recondit"* definitely point to the custody of these records in the church itself or in one of its buildings. Additional evidence of these notaries is found in the section treating of the reign of the successor to Pope Anteros. Pope St. Fabian (236-250) is said to have appointed seven subdeacons who were to have charge of these notaries. These subdeacons were instructed to transcribe the *acta* in full from the *notae* or shorthand methods of the notaries.[5]

More specifically on the topic at hand, the I General Council of Nicaea (325) in its sixteenth canon seemed to postulate some archival system when it legislated regarding the proper diocese for clerics.[6] Lists of the clerics of the diocese as well as records and documents concerning those who were excommunicated must have been kept in some manner of safe, depository or archive. The previous canon of the same Council decreed "that no bishop, priest or deacon should remove from one city to another."[7] A few years after the Council of Nicaea, the Council of Antioch (341) renewed this same prohibition in its twenty-first canon.[8] In fact this rule was later inserted in the

---

[4] *Liber Pontificalis,* I, 147.

[5] *Liber Pontificalis,* I, 148.

[6] "Priests, deacons, or any other clerics who, not having before their eyes the fear of God, nor considering the ecclesiastical law, through a want of earnestness abandon their Church, shall under no condition be received into another Church, but are to be urged by every means to return to their own diocese [παροικίας] ; in case they refuse, they are to be excommunicated (deposed). Should anyone, however, attempt to steal a subject, as it were, who belongs to another (bishop), and, without the consent of the bishop from whom the cleric escaped, ordain him for his own Church, such an ordination shall be invalid."—Schroeder, H. J., *Disciplinary Decrees of the General Councils* (St. Louis: B. Herder Book Co., 1937), p. 46 (hereafter cited as Schroeder); cf. also C. Hefele—Wm. Clark, *A History of the Councils of the Church,* Vol. I (Edinburgh, 2. ed. revised, 1883), p. 423 (hereafter cited as Hefele).

[7] Schroeder, p. 44; Hefele, I, 422.

[8] Mansi, *Sacrorum Conciliorum Nova et Amplissima Collectio* (53 vols. in 60, Parisiis, 1901-1927), II, 1308 (hereafter cited as Mansi).

Corpus Iuris Canonici.[9] While it seems safe to conclude that some archival system was presumed by the Council of Nicaea and the Council of Antioch, it is not inconceivable that an official was needed to arrange and protect these records.

Archbishop Cicognani quotes a verse from the writings of Pope St. Damasus (366-384) to prove the existence of the archives of the Holy See in the fourth century. The archives (*"Cartharium Ecclesiae"*) stood, he says, "where they now stand, namely, in Pompey's Theatre, the site of the present Apostolic Chancery."[10]

St. Augustine (354-430) shortly after this time, in a letter to a group of friends concerning Donatism, quite casually referred to ecclesiastical archives, leading us to believe that archives were in general use in northern Africa in his day.[11]

Actually in 402 the Council of Mileve in Africa distinctly prescribed a *matricula,* or *archivum,* for records of ordination in order to prevent disputes about seniority among the bishops, etc.[12]

The expansion and numerical growth of the Church plus the consequent increase in administrative affairs meant that more and more officials were employed by the bishop to assist with the work. Specialization in these occupations led to various titles. Thus the originally simple office of notary had by this time branched out, causing new names to appear from time to time: *Primicerius, Secundicerius, Chartularius, Scriniarius, Bibliothecarius, Cancellarius, Cubicularius, Syncellus, Conciliarius, Archarius, Nomenclator, etc.*[13]

These titles vary in subsequent periods. In the fifth century the office of notary had apparently reached its zenith in dignity and importance, even in Rome itself. Thus, under Pope St. Leo the Great (440-461) notaries were

---

[9] Cap. XIX, c. VIII, q. 1—Richter-Friedberg, *Corpus Iuris Canonici* (Editio Lipsiensis II, 2 vols., Lipsiae, 1879-1881).

[10] Cicognani, *Canon Law* (2. ed., Reprint, Westminster, Maryland: The Newman Press, 1949), p. 141.

[11] Ep. XLIII, cap. IX—*MPL,* XXXIII, 172.

[12] Canon 86—Mansi, III, 786; cf. also Bingham, *The Antiquities of the Christian Church* (2 vols., London, 1856), I. 62.

[13] Mathias, *The Diocesan Curia* (Madras, India: The Good Pastor Press, 1947), p. 41 (hereafter cited as Mathias).

sent even as legates to Councils.[14] Fifty years earlier, Pope St. Innocent I (402-417) had sent a certain Rufus on a mission, instructing him to be an excellent arbiter. He likewise prescribed that the entire dossier of archival material in the case be turned over to "Sennecius, a very mature priest."[15]

By this time the notaries had formed a college with the *Primicerius* as their head. He was regarded as the head of the papal chancery and was a member of the triumvirate that ruled the Roman Church during a vacancy of the see.[16]

About 475 Acacius, the Patriarch of Constantinople (471-489), when writing to Pope St. Simplicius (468-485) spoke of the papal archives.[17] He used the title *scriniarius,* a title used occasionally for archivist, but apparently never used generally. The word *scrinium* was more often used for the office of the notaries, the chancery. Notaries in general were at times called *scriniarii,* but the title was sometimes used for the notary who worked in the archives. At this time the title *tabularius* was most frequently used in the western half of the Empire, and *chartophylax* was used in the East.[18] These two names were the most specific of the early titles for the archivist.

By the sixth century archives appeared throughout the Church, and they were generally taken for granted in the writings of the period. Constantinople's archives received the most frequent mention.[19] In Africa, Numidia

---

[14] Pelliccia, *De Politia Christianae Ecclesiae* (ed. J. I. Ritter, Coloniae ad Rhenum, 1829), p. 59.

[15] Mansi, VIII, p. 751; Jaffé, *Regesta Pontificum Romanorum ab condita ecclesia ad annum post Christum natum* MCXCVIII (2. ed., G. Wattenbach, F. Kaltenbrunner, P. Ewald, S. Loewenfeld, 2 vols., Lipsiae, 1885-1888), JK, n. 300 (hereafter cited as JK, JE and JL).

[16] This triumvirate or interim government consisted of the archpriest or senior of the Roman priests, the archdeacon, and the *primicerius.* Cf. Rozière, *Liber Diurnus* (Paris, 1869), pp. 108-109, n. 59; also Poole, *Lectures on the History of the Papal Chancery* (Cambridge: Cambridge Press, 1915), p. 17.

[17] *"Sicut enim in nostris archivis inventum est, et de vestris scriniis, si dignamini requirere, poteritis agnoscere, quae in tempore de eodem subsecuta, ab Alexandrino episcopo Romam ad alterutrum sint relata."*—Hardouin, *Acta Conciliorum et Epistolae Decretales ac Constitutiones Summorum Pontificum,* (12 vols., Paris, 1714-1715), II, 805 (hereafter cited as Hardouin).

[18] Louis, *Diocesan Archives,* The Catholic University of America Canon Law Studies, n. 137 (Washington, D. C.: The Catholic University of America Press, 1941), p. 15 (hereafter cited as Louis.)

[19] Mansi, XI, 543, 546, 558, 587; also Hardouin, V, 756, 790.

and Constantina had important acclesiastical archives.[20] The diocesan archives of Arles appeared as early as 529.[21] The archives of Rheims likewise were in existence from an early period.[22].

Article II. Roman Law

In the history of the Roman Law one finds that as early as 367 B. C. a new annual office "was created for the purpose of keeping the state archives."[23] Furthermore, since the primitive law of Rome insisted on the strict observance of prescribed forms, the people had to seek the assistance of legal experts familiar with these forms. "This assistance came from the 'college' of the *pontifices* (pontiffs), a board of priestly officials who maintained an archive in which descriptions of the various rites and phrases were kept on file. Since none but the *pontifices* themselves had access to this archive they were able to preserve a monopoly of legal advice."[24]

Besides, resolutions of the senate were committed to writing and deposited in a special archive (*aerarium*) under the supervision of the quaestors. The plebian *aediles* were later appointed to joint control of the *aerarium* in order to prevent forgery and mishap.[25] Likewise, copies of the imperial rescripts had to be kept, and thus were developed the imperial archives. Interested persons could obtain copies of these rescripts from the imperial archives, and sometimes even from the provincial repositories.[26]

These archives as established in the Roman Law undoubtedly served as norms for the growing administrative procedures of the early Christian Church.

---

[20] Mansi, III, 786.

[21] *Monumenta Germaniae Historica,* Legum Sectio III, *Concilia,* Tomus I, *Concilia Aevi Mervovingici* (recensuit Fridericus Maassen, Hannoverae: Impensis Bibliopolii Hahniani, 1893, p. 53 (hereafter cited as *MGH*).

[22] *MPL,* CXXV, 391.

[23] Wolff,*Roman Law* (Norman, Oklahoma: University of Oklahoma Press, 1951), p. 34 (hereafter cited as Wolff).

[24] Wolff, p. 92.

[25] Jolowicz, *Historical Introduction to the Study of Roman Law* (2. ed., Cambridge: University Press, 1952), p. 43; also Muirhead, *Historical Introduction to the Private Law of Rome* (3. ed., revised and edited by Alexander Grant, London: A. & C. Black, Ltd., 1916), p. 78.

[26] Wolff, p. 86; also Leage, *Roman Private Law* (2. ed. by C. H. Ziegler, London: Macmillan & Co., 1930; reprinted, 1946), p. 15.

Article III. Justinian up to the Council of Trent

The young Church was fortunate, in a way, to have the imperial protection and guidance. And yet an emperor such as Justinian (527-565) was quite capable of excessive zeal. Caesaropapism found its prototype in Justinian. Some of his legislation for the Church, and especially for the clerics, actually was very beneficial and useful. Thus in the question of archives he ordered the erection not only of civil but also of ecclesiastical archives.[27] And he even enacted regulations for the ecclesiastical *chartularii* or custodians of the archives.[28].

Some years later Pope St. Gregory the Great (590-604) mentioned in a letter that the archives of Justinian had been destroyed by fire.[29] It is this same Pope who casually referred to the papal archivist in his letters, and deferred to him as an official of importance. *"Petiistis etenim per Hilarium chartularium nostrum . . ."*[30] In another letter he appointed a commission to handle a case and then added: *"Hujus autem causae exsecutionem Castorio chartulario injungimus, ut ipse nobis debeat cuncta quae acta fuerint, subtiliter renuntiare."*[31] This letter might also be singled out as perhaps the first historical reference that implies a special treatment for a case. The fact that the papal archivist was appointed to report the proceedings accurately to Pope St. Gregory seemed to imply a special concern.

Pope Deusdedit (615-618) in writing to a Spanish Bishop, Gordian, regarding a marriage impediment, stated that he consulted the archives of the Apostolic See and found similar cases cited.[32] This letter with its papal directives was quoted later by Gratian. Apparently it reflects the only mention of archives made in Gratian.[33]

For the next three centuries the extant references were principally to the archives of Constantinople. There, as at Rome, the archivist rose in dignity

---

[27] Nov. (15.5) 2.

[28] C. (1.2) 25; C. (12.49); Nov. (74.4) 2.

[29] *MPL,* LXXVII, 1056.

[30] *MPL,* LXXVII, 531.

[31] *MPL,* LXXVII, 1003.

[32] *Mansi,* X. 536.

[33] C. 1 c. XXX, q. 1.

and importance.[34] The *cartophylax* was mentioned among the members of the secretariate of the Patriarch of Constantinople.[35]

In 805 Charlemagne gave every bishop in his realm the civil power to establish his own notary public, who would be recognized as a public person even in the imperial courts.[36] This episcopal constituting of a notary had an important bearing, for upon his appointment the episcopal notary could present archival material which had value in the civil as well as in the ecclesiastical court. The ecclesiastical notary's position was enhanced thereby. The ecclesiastical archives likewise gained in so far as archival documents could be produced as possessing also an official civil character.

After the time of Charlemagne this power as granted by him to the bishops disappeared, apparently in view of a retraction on the part of Charlemagne's successors. And yet clerics continued to act as notaries.[37] This followed principally from the fact that clerics were the only ones who as a group were able to write. Thus it happened from time to time that the clerics were the only ones available, especially in the smaller communities, to draw up wills, contracts, etc.[38]

This circumstance could lead to abuses, and apparently it did. For in 1211 Pope Innocent III (1198-1216) forbade clerics in Major Orders to hold the office of notary, and threatened excommunication and deprivation or loss of benefice as a sanction.[39]. This severe prohibition was enacted not in consequence of any abuse connected with the archives as such, but rather in view of the conflicts that so easily could arise from those pursuits which, if not unbecoming, were at least foreign to the clerical state. An exception, however, existed in the law. In matters of faith during the Inquisition the court

---

[34] Hardouin, V. 942; Council of Constantinople (1166)—Mansi, XXII, 14; Council of Nymphaeum in Bithynia (1234)—Mansi, XXIII, 299-319.

[35] Mansi, XI, 801.

[36] *MGH, Leges,* I, 131.

[37] A. Bouard, *Manuel de diplomatique française et pontificale* (Paris, 1929), p. 116 (hereafter cited as Bouard).

[38] Cf. Bresslau, *Handbuch der Urkundenlehre für Deutschland und Italien* (2. ed., 2 vols., Leipzig, 1912), I, 593 (hereafter cited as Bresslau); Bouard, p. 116.

[39] C. 8, X, *ne clerici vel monachi saecularibus negotiis se immisceant,* III, 50. Cf. Brunini, *The Clerical Obligations of Canons 139 and 142,* The Catholic University of America Canon Law Studies, n. 103 (Washington, D. C.: The Catholic University of America, 1937), pp. 24-27.

was required strictly to appoint as notaries such clerics who had exercised a notarial office before entering the clerical state. This same law granted permission for all clerics and religious, even those in Sacred Orders, to be public notaries in such cases.[40] Actually, in this period clerics drew up private documents for the people and were "at the same time employed by the bishop in preparing and keeping his documents, whether of ecclesiastical or civil administration, and they were variously and sometimes indiscriminately termed 'chancellor', 'notary' or simply 'secretary'."[41]

The next three centuries added very little to the concepts of notary, archivist or archives. The rise of feudalism in the tenth century did, however, have the effect of developing a diocesan *curia* patterned after the royal chancellery. The notaries employed by the bishops gradually assumed offices similar to those which obtained in the royal curias. Thus evolved the office of chancellor, "the head of the whole documentary system of the diocese."[42] Actually, although indications in the twelfth and thirteenth centuries pointed to the existence of an official whose function was that of archivist-notary, there was still no such legally constituted office in the diocesan curia.

The severe restriction whereby Innocent III forbade clerics to act as notaries was included in the decretal legislation.[43] Decretalists[44] and commentators[45] discussed at some length the question of these notaries as public persons with or without civil standing. At least it appears certain that this prohibition did not forbid clerics to act as public persons in the ecclesiastical curia.[46] Fur-

---

[40] c. 11, *de haereticis,* V, 2, in VI°.

[41] Prince, *The Diocesan Chancellor,* The Catholic University of America Canon Law Studies, n. 167 (Washington, D. C.: The Catholic University of America Press, 1942), pp. 14-15 (hereafter cited as Prince).

[42] Prince, p. 18; cf. also Monin, *De Curia Romana* (Louvain, 1912), p. 121, for his brief history of the Apostolic Chancery.

[43] C. 8, X, *ne clerici vel monachi saecularibus negotiis se immisceant,* III, 50.

[44] E. g., Fagnanus, *Commentarium in decretalium libros* (5 vols., Venetiis, 1709), III, 651-659.

[45] Lega-Bartoccetti, *Commentarius in Iudicia Ecclesiastica iuxta Codicem Iuris Canonici* (3 vols., Romae: Anonima Libraria Cattolica Italiana, 1950, I, 147 (hereafter cited as *Commentarius*); Bouix, *Tractatus de Iudiciis Ecclesiasticis* (2 vols., Parisiis, 1855), I, 482-496; De Lugo, *Disputationes de iustitia et de iure* (2. ed., 2 vols., Venetiis, 1718), Vol. II, disp. XLI, sec. II, pp. 443-445.

[46] Wernz-Vidal, *Ius Canonicum ad Codicis Normam Exactum* (7 vols. in 8, Vol. II, *De Personis,* 3 ed., a P. Aguirre, Romae: Apud Aedes Universitatis Gregorianae, 1943), pp. 814-815 (hereafter cited as Wernz-Vidal).

thermore, these notaries went by various names such as *actuarii, tabelliones, cancellarii,* and these terms were used interchangeably from the thirteenth century onward. Only the latter title was destined to continue in use, and the practice whereby this chancellor became the custodian of the archives led to particular legal enactments, and eventually to the general law of the Code, as setting up the office of chancellor with the double function in the curia of archivist and public notary.[47].

Archives evidently were in existence from the earliest times. Though no detailed legislation was enacted on the matter, yet it appears certain that general norms of administration dictated the actual use of archives in the course of the first sixteen centuries of ecclesiastical history. In fact, Barraclough finds the character of the Church expressed particularly in its day-to-day business and in its care for the small matters of government. In his analysis of the Church in the middle ages he claims that "in the general history of the Church no factor is of greater importance, as an index of decline or of progress, than the history of government and administration."[48]

For tracing the development leading up to precise ecclesiastical legislation on the secret archives of the curia, it has been necessary to consider the evidences of history in both Roman law and ecclesiastical writings. With the growth in administrative affairs the curial officials of Rome and of other sections of the ecclesiastical world found it imperative to enlarge their archival systems, and to utilize greater safeguards for the increase of documents in the various repositories.

---

[47] Can. 372.

[48] Barraclough, *Papal Provisions* (Oxford: Basil Blackwell, 1935), pp. 1-4.

CHAPTER II

HISTORICAL DEVELOPMENT FROM THE SIXTEENTH CENTURY

Article I. Tridentine and Papal Influence

The general and ecumenical Council of Trent (1545-1563), convoked during the pontificate of Pope Paul III (1534-1549), had the twofold purpose of the genuine and thorough reform of Catholic life and the definite statement of the Church's doctrine as a reply to the heresies of Protestantism. The administrative control over the universal Church was profoundly threatened by the so-called reforms as well as by the weaknesses and vices that polluted even the clergy of the sixteenth century. The Tridentine Fathers strove valiantly to restore ecclesiastical discipline and authority in the Church.

Because the issues at stake were so varied and so specific, the merely procedural questions were of secondary importance. Hence no legislation on archives appeared in the decrees of the Council of Trent. And yet the existence and use of archives were implied in various decrees, particularly in the regulations concerning notaries. As in so many other ecclesiastical institutes, incompetency was found in the notarial system. Thus the accuracy of records and of documents were easily jeopardized by such abuse of office.

In order to correct these difficulties, the Council of Trent gave the bishop the powers necessary to insure competency in his notaries. The decree reads as follows:

> Since the incompetency of notaries causes very much harm and is the occasion of many lawsuits, the bishop, also as delegate of the Apostolic See, may by examination inquire into the fitness of all notaries, even though appointed by Apostolic, imperial or royal authority; and if found incompetent or at any time delinquent in office, he may forbid them either altogether or for a time to exercise the office in ecclesiastical and spiritual affairs, lawsuits and causes. No appeal on their part shall suspend the prohibition of the ordinary.[1]

---

[1] Sess. XXII, *de. ref.*, c. 10: "*Cum ex notariorum imperitia plurima damna et multarum occasio litium oriatur, possit episcopus quoscumque notarios, etiamsi apostolica, imperiali aut regia auctoritate creati fuerint, etiam tamquam delegatus Sedis Apostolicae, examina-*

While the decrees of the Council of Trent were often quite specific, as in the decree just cited, the Council's influence is especially noted in the synodal legislation subsequent to the general council. Thus St. Charles Borromeo (1538-1584), Cardinal-archbishop of Milan, stated quite plainly that he convoked the I Provincial Council of Milan (1565) to put into effect the decrees of the Council of Trent.[2] Furthermore, the Milan Councils themselves, six within seventeen years, were to exercise great influence on the particular laws passed in other places by bishops who followed the lead of St. Charles.

The first papal legislation, albeit particular, on diocesan archives appeared eight years after the Council of Trent adjourned. In his Constitution "*Muneris Nostri*" (1571) Pope St. Pius V (1566-1572) stated very bluntly that his reason for writing this directive to the bishops of Sicily was the existence of deplorable conditions in that country whereby there had been serious loss of testimonies and *acta* of criminal cases. He demanded an authentic inventory as a guarantee against future losses. He further decreed that the bishop, when he foresaw his approaching death, was by testament to commit the custody of these archives to his confessor or to a monastery until his successor was appointed. Also, any cleric who removed or in any way destroyed material from the archives was to be deprived of his dignity, office or benefice, and thereafter held as incapacitated (*inhabilis*) for any dignity, office or benefice.[3]

A few years later, Pope Sixtus V (1585-1590) in his Constitution *Provida* commanded the erection of archives in each diocese, Order or pious place of Italy.[4]

---

tione adhibita eorum sufficientiam scrutari, illisque non idoneis repertis, aut quandocumque in officio delinquentibus, officii ejus in negotiis, litibus et causis ecclesiasticis ac spiritualibus exercendi usum perpetuo aut ad tempus prohibere. Neque eorum appellatio interdictionem ordinarii suspendat." Use is made of the translation of the text of the Council by Schroeder (1875-1942) in his *Canons and Decrees of the Council of Trent* (St. Louis: Herder, 1941), pp. 158 and 430. Cf. also Duerr, *The Judicial Notary,* The Catholic University of America Canon Law Studies, n. 332 (Washington, D. C.: The Catholic University of America Press, 1951), p. 26 (hereafter cited as Duerr).

[2] Ratti (Pope Pius XI), *Acta Ecclesiae Mediolanensis* (3 vols., Milan, 1890-1892), II, p. 158; cf. also Hardouin, X, 633.

[3] Pius V, const. *Muneris Nostri,* 1 mart. 1581—*Bullarum Diplomatum et Privilegiorum Romanorum Pontificum Taurinensis Editio,* (24 vols. et Appendix, Augustae Taurinorum, 1857-1872), VII, 893 (hereafter cited as *Bullarium Romanum*).

[4] Sixtus V, const. *Provida,* 29 apr. 1587, found in Appendix VIII, *Concilium Romanum (1725)*, p. 178. Cf. also Quaranta, *Summa Bullarii Earumve Summorum Pontificum Constitutionum* (Venetiis, 1622), vide "Archivus", p. 88.

The next papal legislation on archives was again addressed to all local ordinaries of Italy and its adjacent islands. The constitution *Maxima vigilantia,* issued June 14, 1727, was the most thorough and precise treatment until the publication of the Code, and has since its appearance served as the model for most of the local legislation and stands as the principal source cited in the Code for the canons on archives.[5]

Sixteen years later Benedict XIV (1740-1758) issued his Constitution *Satis Vobis* in order to regulate marriages of conscience. In it one can trace the first juridicial vestige of the institute of secret archives. The very nature of these marriages postulated secrecy as a protection, and accordingly one finds for the first time a specific element in the universal legislation on secret archives.[6]

Not until 1913 was there any further papal legislation on archives. Pius X (1903-1914) issued new regulations for the Vicariate of Rome on January 1, 1912. Setting up four departments in the curia, he decreed two archives for each department, a secret archive and a general archive.[7]

These five papal constitutions will be considered more in detail in the following articles. For the present it may be observed that local conciliar legislation during the post-Tridentine period relied greatly on the initial regulations sponsored by St. Charles Borromeo as well as on the above-mentioned papal constitutions.

It seems strange that, although the Council of Trent demanded that metropolitans convoke provincial councils at least once every three years,[8] these councils were held only infrequently during the three centuries subsequent to

---

[5] Benedictus XIII, const. *Maxima vigilantia,* 14 iun. 1727—*Bullarium Romanum,* XXII, 560-567; cf. also *Codicis Iuris Canonici Fontes,* cura Emi Petri Card. Gasparii editi (9 vols., Romae [postea Civitate Vaticana]: Typis Polyglottis Vaticanis, 1923-1939), n. 293; also Lucidi, *De Visitatione Sacrorum Liminium* (3. ed., 3 vols., Romae, 1883), III, 164.

[6] Benedictus XIV, const. *Satis Vobis,* 17 nov. 1741—*Fontes,* n. 319. Cf. Ayrinhac-Lydon, *Marriage Legislation in the New Code of Canon Law* (rev. ed., New York: Benziger Brothers, 1949), pp. 281-285 (hereafter cited as Ayrinhac-Lydon); cf. also Wernz-Vidal, II, p. 819, n. 648.

[7] Pius X, const. *Etsi Nos,* 1 ian. 1912—*Fontes,* n. 697.

[8] Cf. sess. XXIV, *de ref.,* c. 2; Schroeder, p. 462.

the Council of Trent. But within the second half of the past century councils once again became a vital part in the shaping of ecclesiastical discipline.[9]

Article II. Erection of the Archives

Very many of the diocesan and provincial councils seemed to presume the existence of archives, but most of them specifically commanded their erection by the local ordinaries. Two years after the Council of Trent the Council of Toledo (1565) stated quite categorically: "*Episcopi publicum archivum habeant* . . ."[10] At this early date it is remarkable to find such a pioneer council give precise and detailed legislation regarding these archives. The content matter, decreed the Council, was to be placed in the safest custody possible.[11] Furthermore, the bishop was to erect these archives in a monastery either in his see city, or elsewhere in the diocese if he found it more expedient. And for their safer protection two keys were prescribed, so that when the see became vacant one key was to be given by the bishop's vicar general to one of the chapter members or one deputed by the chapter, and the other key to the prelate of the monastery where the archives were. The latter was required to take an oath that he would faithfully guard his key, and further that he would not permit any document to be removed from the archives without the permission of the metropolitan or the latter's superior. In this same decree the bishops were admonished to be mindful of the oath they took at the time of their consecration regarding the alienation of ecclesiastical goods, and that any neglect of ecclesiastical documents could involve them in the guilt of alienation.

These points are mentioned here, first of all in indication of the great care shown at this early date for archival material, and then also of the accuracy of this early conciliar legislation. One cannot assume, however, that this high degree of discipline was universal. Ouly a few years later, as has already been seen, Pius V found it necessary to complain in his *Muneris Nostri* (1571) of the grave loss of documents with reference to tribunal cases.

The third of the provincial councils of Milan was held in 1573. While the two previous councils seemed to presuppose that diocesan archives were

---

[9] Popek, *The Rights and Obligations of Metropolitans,* The Catholic University of America Canon Law Studies, n. 260 (Washington, D. C.: The Catholic University of America Press, 1947), p. 119.

[10] Council of Toledo (1565)—Hardouin, X, 1158.

[11] "*In tutissimam custodiam deponantur.*"—Hardouin, X, 1158.

already in existence, the third decreed that a special section of the episcopal archive was to be erected for the safekeeping of the matters connected with judicial trials. And this particular archive was to be locked with two keys, one being in the possession of the bishop, and the other in the hands of the chancellor. This seems the first legislation that called for a particularized archive, or an archive within an archive. An additional requirement for the archives of the cathedral chapters was the keeping of a special book describing the properties and rights of the churches of the whole diocese. A unique ordinance with reference to this last archive was the demand that it be locked by means of three keys. This appears to be the only known instance of a law requiring more than two keys for any archive.[12]

The Council of Rome (1725) included in its appendix a "Catalog of the writings which must be preserved in the archives of the episcopal curia." Among these writings all the *acta* and documents pertaining to matters of the Holy Office were to be preserved in a separate and locked archive. Here is perhaps the first precise reference in legislation to a secret archive, but the reference is such as to imply that such archives already existed.[13]

In the same year the Council of Avignon (1725) urged the bishops of the province to serve as an example for others in the matter of establishing and maintaining the required archives.[14] It is noteworthy that this Council cited as one of its sources the Council of Rome, which had been held only a few months earlier.

Pope Benedict XIII in his constitution *Maxima vigilantia* (1727) reflected his conviction regarding the necessity of additional statutes beyond the ones enacted by Pius V in 1571. He remarked that he himself, when he was Archbishop of Benevento some thirty years previously, had tried to follow the lead of the Councils and Pontiffs in commanding the erection of archives for the preservation and protection of documents. Now, as Supreme Pontiff, he reiterated this legislation for all of Italy.[15]

---

[12] III Council of Milan (1573), Decr. XVIII, n. V—Hardouin, X, 795.

[13] Council of Rome (1725), Appendix XI, sec. III, n. 9, p. 193.

[14] Council of Avignon (1725)—*Acta et Decreta Sacrorum Conciliorum Recentiorum, Collectio Lacensis* (7 vols., Friburgi Brisgoviae, 1870-1892), II, 579 (hereafter cited as *Coll Lac.*).

[15] Benedictus XIII, const. *Maxima vigilantia,* 14 iun. 1727, nn. 1-3—*Bullarium Romanum,* XXII, 560; *Fontes,* n. 293.

Among the Orientals the Maronites held an important council at Mount Lebanon in 1736. In this council their bishops were bidden to erect archives in their cathedral churches.[16] Archbishop Cicognani notes that of the synods proper to each of the Oriental Churches "this Synod is considered more perfect and elaborate than the others."[17] There will be occasion later to consider some of the details of this legislation.

The constitution *Satis Vobis* (1741) of Benedict XIV, in laying down the conditions on which marriages of conscience could be permitted, demanded that the pastor or the priest who assisted at such marriages send a written report of them to the ordinary. These documents were to be transcribed, word for word, in a special book which was to be kept in the secret archives of the diocese. As in the Council of Rome (1725) some years previously, the existence of diocesan secret archives was presupposed, and thus one may assume that for some time they had been in existence, and constituted part and parcel of the curial furniture and equipment.[18].

The Bishops of Ireland in the Plenary Council of Thurles (1850), lamenting the ruin and the loss of records and documents, required each diocese to have an archive in a very safe and convenient place.[19]

The Council of Ravenna (1855) repeated the provisions of the III Provincial Council of Milan (1573) almost verbatim in requiring a special archive for the material relating to the tribunal.[20]

The Provincial Council of Urbino (1859) required every college of canons to have an archive according to the norms of the Council of Rome (1725).[21]

Three kinds of archives were distinguished by the Council of Lucca (1887): the archiepiscopal archives for metropolitan matters, the archbishop's private archives, and the archives of the curia. Specific mention was made of a secret archive within the latter two archives.[22]

---

[16] Council of Mount Lebanon (1736)—*Coll. Lac.*, II, 329.

[17] Cicognani, p. 448.

[18] Benedictus XIV, *Satis Vobis,* 17 nov. 1741—*Fontes,* n. 319; cf. also Ayrinhac-Lydon, pp. 281-285.

[19] Decr. XXI: "*in loco quo possit tutiori simul et commodiori . . .*"—*Coll. Lac.*, III, 793.

[20] Council of Ravenna (1855), Pars IV, cap. IX, n. IX—*Coll. Lac.*, VI, 211.

[21] Council of Urbino (1859), Pars II, tit. III, n. CXXIII—*Coll. Lac.*, VI. 42.

[22] *Lucanae Ecclesiae Synodus Dioecesana* (Lucae, 1887), Cap. VI, nn. I-III, p. 307.

Thus it is evident that between the Council of Trent and the promulgation of the Code diocesan archives, and especially secret archives, became an integral part of diocesan administration. The next logical step was inevitable, namely the enactment of universal legislation requiring secret archives in every diocesan curia. The Code in enacting such legislation cited as its principal sources the two papal Constitutions *Satis Vobis* of Benedict XIV and *Etsi Nos* of Pius X.

Article III. Contents of the Archives

At first the councils that commanded the erection of diocesan archives treated of the contents of these archives in general terms. Thus the Council of Toledo (1565) and several subsequent councils required that any and all writings pertaining to the episcopal office, its rights and transactions, be placed in the archives.[23]

But the influence which derived from the papal Constitution *Muneris Nostri* (1571) of Pius V and from the enactments incorporated by St. Charles Borromeo in the III Provincial Council of Milan (1573) led to a more specific legislation in this matter. The Constitution *Muneris Nostri* sought to counteract the loss of testimony and of documents relating to criminal cases.[24] In line with this solicitude, the Milanese Council went a step further by decreeing a special archive for the preservation of all judicial matters.[25]

The Council of Mexico (1585) added an interesting requirement. Royal grants, commissions and appointments were to be preserved as archival material. In consequence of Spanish conquest in the New World, these royal grants were generally very important, inasmuch as duly vindicated property rights, properly acknowledged ecclesiastical and even civil exemptions from the local representative of Spain, and the offered royal pledges of support were important factors for the new institutions founded under the Spanish flag.[26]

Some councils drew up a list, demonstrative rather than comprehensive, of the documents and materials to be preserved in the archives. The Council of Mexico (1585) was one of the first to incorporate such a list. The Council

---

[23] Council of Toledo (1565)—Hardouin, X, 1158; I Council of Benevento (1693)—*Coll. Lac.*, I, 103; Council of Turin (1849)—*Coll. Lac.*, IV, 266; Council of Bordeaux (1850)—*Coll. Lac.*, IV, 586; Council of Bourges (1850)—*Coll. Lac.*, IV. 1132.

[24] *Bullarium Romanum*, VII, 893-894.

[25] III Provincial Council of Milan (1573)—Hardouin, X, 795.

[26] Hardouin, X, 1677.

of Naples (1699) lengthened the list with more specific items, such as inventories of all the goods, movable and immovable, belonging to churches and ecclesiastical benefices; pious legacies and documents pertaining thereto; and all established rights and claims vesting in the ecclesiastical tribunal and centering in the goods and revenues of the cathedral *mensa*.[27]

The Council of Rome (1725) quoted verbatim in its appendix the long list given by the Council of Benevento (1693), but made two additions, the second of which is of great importance to the matter at hand. This was the requirement that all recorded acts and documents relating to matters pertaining to the Holy Office should be preserved in a separate and locked archive. Historically, this is the first legislative determination of the contents of the secret archives.[28]

The spirit as well as the scope of all this legislation was succintly described in the Council of Lucca (1887): *"Et scripturae quae accuratiorem custodiam postulant, in secretiori loco, clave munito, recondantur."*[29]

Canon 379, § 1, in the Code has in the same way abstracted from presenting any comprehensive list of the matters to be associated with the secret archives, for it states quite simply: *"in eo scripturae secreto servandae cautissime custodiantur."*[30]

Article IV. Custody of the Archives

It is remarkable that so soon after the Council of Trent a council in Spain issued such precise and thorough legislation as one finds in the Council of Toledo (1565). Documents and writings of the bishop's office were to be placed in his archives and the safest custody possible given them—*"In tutissimam custodiam deponantur."* Furthermore, no original document was to be taken out of the archives except for the reason that strict justice required it or that some accruing advantage for the bishop's office or the Church warranted it.

The archives were to be erected in a monastery, manifestly with a view to the guarantee of safety. Two keys were needed for entry into these archives, so that when the see was vacant there would be effectively forestalled every attempt to tamper with the archives. One of these keys was to be held by a member of the chapter, the other by the superior of the monastery housing

---

[27] Tit. XII, c. II, n. 7—*Coll. Lac.*, I, 238.

[28] *Concilium Romanum* (*1725*), Appendix XI, sec. III, n. 9., p. 139; Council of Benevento (1693), Appendix V—*Coll. Lac.*, I, 103.

[29] *Lucanae Ecclesiae Synodus Dioecesana*, Cap. VI, n. II, p. 308.

the archives. This latter superior had to promise under oath that during the vacancy nothing would be withdrawn from the archives except with the permission of the metropolitan or his superior.

A biennial visitation of the archives was enjoined on the bishop. In order to indicate the gravity of the bishop's responsibility with regard to the archives, the decree pointed out that the bishops of the province should be mindful of the oath, taken by them at their consecration, not to alienate church property, and that they would be guilty of such alienation, if, through their negligence, the very documents which protected the goods and the rights of the Church should be lost. All these regulations as made on behalf of the diocesan archives were applied also to archives of cathedral or collegiate churches.[80]

In the light of such careful legislation, almost immediately after the reforms of the Council of Trent, it is no wonder that subsequent legislation regarding the custody of ecclesiastical documents would repeat most of these precautions and adapt them to local conditions.

The III Provincial Council of Milan (1573) added two special safeguards. If the chancellor or one of the notaries died or resigned or was removed from office, then whatever documents or records were in his possession at the time were to be placed immediately in the archives at the order of the bishop. But if the procedural acts of a case were among those and the parties wished to continue the prosecution of the case, it was permitted to withhold these documents from the archives until the case was completed. The second safeguard was the further determination of responsibility in the event of the bishop's death. In such a case the vicar-general was directed to remove all documents and records from the bishop's private archives and place them in the diocesan archives. If anyone interfered with this duty of the vicar-general, the penalty was a *latae sententiae* major excommunication, and if the chapter itself interfered, it was subject to an interdict.

These two precautions give clear evidence of the determined efforts of the Church to protect and defend its archives. Perhaps because there were more individuals involved in a cathedral chapter, the Council demanded three keys for the capitular archives, thereby attempting to forestall collusion between the chapter members who held the keys to the archives. While one or two might

---

[80] Council of Toledo (1565), Act. III, cap. 1—Hardouin, X, 1158.

be persuaded to tamper with the archival material, it was less likely that three of the canons would violate their trust simultaneously.[31]

All this legislation, however, did not guarantee observance, and so it is hardly surprising that the II Council of Benevento (1698) found it necessary to deplore flagrant violations. This council complained that no account was paid to Pius V's Constitution *Muneris Nostri,* the ordinances of which the previous Council of Benevento (1693) had urgently stressed. The Council pointed to a case within the province wherein, during the vacancy of one of the sees, some persons had seized the episcopal archives, and those who were bound to protect the archives had let this crime pass unnoticed. With a view to covering up this crime, the perpetrators had in addition hidden the documents. Accordingly the council commanded all the bishops to seek out the culprits, their accomplices and the notary involved, and to punish them according to the norms given in the Constitution *Muneris Nostri,* thus setting an example that would dissuade further violations in this matter.[32]

The Council of Naples (1699) was not satisfied with committing the custody of the archives to the bishops in a general way. In order to stress the importance of this custody, the Council demanded that the archivist be a specifically designated and reliable individual—"*custodia certo fidelique viro committatur.*"[33]

This Council likewise enacted some strict norms for the proper exercise of his office on the part of the archivist. He was forbidden to give his archive keys to anyone. He could not permit anyone to examine any of the documents except in his presence. He could not give copies of any of the archival documents unless permission had been obtained from the vicar-general. And he could never loan any original documents except with the vicar-general's permission, which could be granted only to ecclesiastics of that city or diocese. For the violation of this latter regulation the archivist could be punished with incarceration or some other severe penalty. If permission was granted for the borrowing of any documents, this had to be noted in a special book, and the documents had to be returned within fifteen days.[34]

---

[31] III Council of Milan (1573), Decr. XVIII, n. V-VII—Hardouin, X, 795.

[32] II Council of Benevento (1698), Tit. I, cap. II—*Coll. Lac.,* I, 129.

[33] Tit. XII, cap. II, n. 6—*Coll, Lac.,* I, 238.

[34] Council of Naples (1699), Tit. XII, cap. II, nn. 10-11—*Coll. Lac.,* I, 238.

The Council of Rome (1725) likewise stressed explicit details in its legislation concerning the custody of the archives. Again there was an expression of concern for the safety of these archives upon the bishop's death, and the bishops were reminded of their serious duty to invoke the needed safeguards in this respect.[85]

The Council of Avignon (1725) called attention in particular to the bishop's obligation to seek out the lost and recover the scattered documents especially with reference to the cases pending in the diocesan tribunal, for in such procedures a loss of the documents could so easily result through carelessness in the matter of seeking to recover them.[86]

In many of the Councils, *inventaria* or detailed descriptive lists of all the archival material were required. These *inventaria* were more comprehensive than mere substantial lists, for they included a detailed and itemized description of the contents of the documents. The Council of Fermo (1726) demanded a special care for these *inventaria.* Annually they were to be brought up to date to include all the additions made to the archives. The importance of these *inventaria* was evident, for by means of them the contents of the archives could easily be determined. Accordingly, these *inventaria* needed strict protection against possible tampering. That explained why such detailed regulations were invoked for the safeguarding of these *inventaria* if the bishop died or was absent from his diocese for a long time. The cathedral chapter, even before electing the vicar capitular, had to visit the archives and draw up a new *inventarium* according to the contents of the archives at the time. The new *inventarium* was then to be compared with the one left by the bishop, and both were to be filed in the archives.[87]

The Maronite Council of Mount Lebanon (1736) added an interesting regulation. Lest any of the procedural acts be lost or become unavailable when needed, the notary was within two months from the completion of a case to turn the entire *acta* over to the archivist, so that all the acts of the case might be preserved in the archives.[88]

The matters relating to marriages of conscience demanded complete secrecy because of the grave reasons for which these marriages were permitted. But

---

[85] *Concilium Romanum* (1725), Tit. XII, cap. IV, p. 41.

[86] Council of Avignon (1725), Tit. XLVI, cap. 1—*Coll. Lac.,* I, 579.

[87] Council of Fermo (1726), Tit. VI—*Coll. Lac.,* I, 595.

[88] Council of Mount Lebanon (1736), Pars III, cap. V, n. 10—*Coll. Lac.,* II, 332.

in order to prevent the emergence of abuses from this special canonical institute, Benedict XIV in his Constitution *Satis Vobis* (1741) gave explicit directions in protection of those who had received permission to use this privilege. This Constitution is of profound importance for the Code legislation, not only in that it concerns the procedure in connection with the marriage of conscience, but also in that it so carefully reveals the scope which the secret archives must serve. By analogy, the handling of similar matters of secrecy could definitely look to this Constitution for hints regarding points of procedure to be followed and elements of care to be expended.[39]

The Council of Ravenna (1855) urged bishops to be mindful of the fact that the very name of bishop signified that they were watchmen placed over the house of Israel, and correspondingly warned them to be vigilant in the performance of their duties and in the exercise of their obligations. It then added that bishops need to be zealous in their care of the archives, regardless of their character as episcopal, capitular or parochial archives.[40]

The chancellor as archivist made his appearance in legislation for the first time in 1573 in the decrees of the III Provincial Council of Milan. Some later councils spoke of the archivist under the title of secretary.[41] and others designated him simply as the custodian.[42] But the Council of Urbino (1859) was one of the first important councils to refer to the chancellor specifically as the archivist for the episcopal archives.[43] The III Plenary Council of Baltimore (1884) pointed out that the chancellor as archivist contributes much to the proper and prompt functioning of diocesan business.[44]

Unusually exacting precautions were enacted at the Council of Lucca (1887). The priest in charge of the archiepiscopal archives was required to draw up an index of all the documents contained in those archives. The chancellor was to do the same for the archives of the curia. Two priests, appointed by the Council, were to compare these indexes with the actual documents in the archives, and present a report of their findings to the archbishop the while a

---

[39] Benedictus XIV, const. *Satis Vobis,* 17 nov. 1741—*Fontes,* n. 319.
[40] Council of Ravenna (1855), Pars IV, cap. I, n. III—*Cqll. Lac.,* VI, 211.
[41] E. g., the Council of Rouen (1589), n. 9—Hardouin, X, 1255.
[42] E. g., the Council of Naples (1699), cap. II, n. 10—*Coll. Lac.,* I, 238.
[43] Council of Urbino (1859), Pars II, tit. IV, n. CXXVII—*Coll. Lac.,* VI, 43; cf. also Prince, pp. 24-33.
[44] III Plenary Council of Baltimore (1884), *Acta et Decreta,* n. 271, p. 155.

copy of this report was placed in the archives. Annually these two priests together with the vicar-general were to visit the archives and again compare the indexes with the documents. If anything was out of order, they were to report it to the archbishop. These strict regulations were not incorporated in the Code, and it will be necessary later to study the question in greater detail in order to determine if such extremes may ever be warranted today.

The development of jurisprudence regarding the custody of the archives had been comparatively slight, but the principle involved never lost its impact and vigor. What was important in the history of the custody of the archives was the ready response on the part of ecclesiastical authority to cope with the problems as they arose. There were forthright attempts, made not only by the Roman Pontiffs but also by subordinate legislators, to enact laws to meet the current exigencies. It was events such as the Roman Pontiff's exile in Avignon and the recurring wars in the Papal States that entailed the transfer of archives from place to place, on repeated occasions, and unquestionably to the detriment of the proper safekeeping and safeguarding of the archives.[45]

Article V. Use of the Archives

Essential to a good administration in respect of the archives was the care and the caution employed for the guaranteeing of an adequate but controlled use of the archival material. In line with the importance of the documents, greater or lesser precautions were required in the use to which the documents were subjected. Therefore, it is not surprising to find explicit legislation on this point almost simultaneously with the general legislation on archives.

The Council of Toledo (1565) showed concern particularly for original documents. It forbade the taking of any original document from the archives except for a very grave reason (*"ex ea causa quae justissima sit"*) that militated in favor of the utility of the Church. Furthermore, these original documents could be withdrawn only if two witnesses and a notary were present, and the notary made note of this withdrawal in the *inventarium,* together with the information concerning what was taken, by whom, and why. If the see was

---

[45] Cf. Cerchiari, *Cappellani Papae et Apostolicae Sedis, Auditores Causarum Sacri Palatii Apostolici seu S. R. Rotae, ab Origine ad Diem usque 20 sept., 1870* (4 vols., Romae, 1919-1921), Vol. III, p. X, for his brief history of the Secret Archives of the Rota.

vacant, no document whatever could be withdrawn from the archives except with the permission of the metropolitan or his superior.[46]

Special consideration was accorded the documents pertaining to judicial procedure and to cases pending in court. The III Provincial Council of Milan (1573), besides demanding that a special section of the episcopal archives be set aside for tribunal cases ("*certus in archivo episcopali locus constituatur*"), wanted these documents kept in such a fashion as would permit their ready use if they were needed again in the tribunal ("*ita ut inde, cum usuvenerit, promi possit quidquid in ecclesiastico foro umquam agitatum erit.*")[47]

The Council of Mexico (1585) repeated the restrictions enacted in the Council of Toledo (1565), except for the fact that no distinction was made that lent any added favor in respect of original documents. The Mexican Council subjected to the same restrictions all archival documents, whether originals or mere copies of originals.[48]

The Council of Naples (1699) not only demanded, as did the earlier councils, that documents from the archives could be examined only in the presence of the archivist, but added also some specific requirements about the removal of these documents. Even copies of documents could not be withdrawn except with the permission of the vicar-general. The use of original documents or of procedural acts upon their removal from the archives required the written permission of the vicar-general, and a loan of this kind could be made only in favor of ecclesiastics. Whenever these documents were loaned, note of this had to be made in a special register in the archives, and the borrowed document had to be returned within fifteen days.[49]

Documents removed from the archives could easily be lost or through forgetfulness remain unreturned. In adverting to this the Council of Avignon (1725) warned the bishops, and called upon them to exercise all care and concern to recover such documents.[50] This admonition was repeated by Pope Benedict XIII in his Constitution *Maxima vigilantia* (1727). He further demanded that, if a document was legitimately withdrawn, it could not be kept

---

[46] Council of Toledo (1565), Act. III, cap. I—Hardouin, X, 1158.
[47] III Council of Milan (1573), Decr. XVIII—Hardouin, X, 795.
[48] Council of Mexico (1585), Lib. III, tit. VIII, n. VI—Hardouin, X, 1677.
[49] Council of Naples (1699), Tit. XII, cap. II, nn. 10-11—*Coll. Lac.*, I, 238.
[50] Council of Avignon (1725), Tit. XLVI, cap. I—*Coll. Lac.*, I, 579.

for more than three days, which was a considerable restriction in comparison with the fifteen days permitted by the Council of Naples (1699). But it must be remembered that Benedict XIII had, in his introductory remarks to this Constitution, pointed out the valiant efforts of previous legislation, and his present concern was to remove serious abuses.[51]

The Maronites demanded in their Council of Mount Lebanon (1736) that the bishop be the only one to grant permission for the borrowing of original documents from the archives, and he was to exact a testimony of the granted loan from the person borrowing the document. Although there must have been knowledge of Benedict XIII's stringent regulation for only a three-day use of the documents, nevertheless the fifteen-day period was invoked in the conciliar legislation. But the Council did accept the regular norm that documents could be examined only in the presence of the archivist.[52].

It was certainly imperative that precise legislation control the use of information regarding marriages of conscience. And so Benedict XIV described three conditions under which the bishop would be justified in opening and inspecting the special register kept for this purpose in the secret archives. The three conditions were: 1) That he be called on to enter the record of other such marriages in the register; 2) that for the proper administration of justice he needed to inspect the secret register, and 3) that for truly interested parties there was a need of a document without which desired proofs and evidence could not be obtained elsewhere. But in all cases the bishops were warned to be careful to return the register promptly to its secret place. The Pope made it clear, however, that information taken from this register, whether of the marriage or of the baptism of the children of such a marriage, was to be accorded the same faith and trustworthiness as was accorded to information drawn from any other archive record.[53].

The Council of Ravenna (1855) stated briefly and to the point that the episcopal archives were to be kept up-to-date and in good and neat order, so that if and when anything was needed it could be produced. None of the earlier more stringent measures were included among the enactments of this Council, which was perhaps an indication that the previously faced difficulties had either subsided or had been counteracted.[54]

---

[51] Benedictus XIII, *Maxima vigilantia,* 14 iun. 1727—*Fontes,* n. 293.

[52] Council of Mount Lebanon (1736), Pars III, cap. IV, n. 37—*Coll. Lac.,* II, 329.

[53] Benedictus XIV, const. *Satis Vobis,* 17 nov. 1741, § 10—*Fontes,* n. 319.

[54] Council of Ravenna (1855), Para IV, cap. IX, n. IX—*Coll. Lac.,* VI, 211.

Nevertheless a few years later the Council of Lucca (1887) enacted very detailed legislation that harked back to the stricter norms of earlier times. The archivist of the archdiocesan archives was forbidden to let anyone examine archival material of any kind unless permission had been received from the archbishop or his vicar-general. It was absolutely forbidden to borrow any document; the only thing that anyone could do was to read the document in the presence of the archivist. Similar restrictions were placed on the archivist, or secretary, of the private archives of the archbishop, as also on the chancellor in regard to the curial archives.[55]

The use of the archives definitely demanded some safeguards. It has been seen how local legislation varied from time to time to meet the contemporary needs. But in all that was done there was evidence that the Church consistently sought, on the one hand, to protect important secret matters against harmful divulgement, and, on the other, to allow a just and equitable use of this material when knowledge of it became an essential demand.

Article VI.— Penalties for Violations of Laws Concerning the Archives

The rampant upheavals in the wake of the Protestant revolt plus the abuses found even among responsible members of the true Church made it necessary for the Church to use strong and at times severe penal sanctions in order to check the disastrous evils. Hence it was almost to be expected that one would find the incumbent of the Chair of Peter among the first and most adamant legislators in this matter. Pope St. Pius V in his important Constitution *Muneris Nostri* (1571) not only deplored the serious malice inherent in the theft, destruction, alteration and falsification of official documents, but decreed grave penalties in order to correct these evils. With the plenitude of his apostolic authority he threatened the forfeiture of authoritative status of office and of benefice to anyone who removed or destroyed documents relating to criminal trials. He threatened the same penalties for notaries who abused their office by falsifying the documents.[56]

This papal enactment, though it was addressed to the bishops of Sicily as particular legislation, nevertheless proved influential in almost all the subsequent legislation that adverted to penal sanctions for violators of the law here in question.

---

[55] *Lucanae Ecclesiae Synodus Dioecesana,* Cap. VI, nn. I-III, pp. 307-308.
[56] Pius V, *Muneris Nostri,* 1 mart. 1571—*Bullarium Romanum,* VII, 893-894.

The III Council of Milan (1573) was one of the first Councils to decree penalties for violations of the law regarding archives. The particular concern of this Council seemed to attach to that period of time following immediately upon the death of a bishop. In order to protect the archives, the Council commanded the vicar-general to transfer all documents and registers from the deceased bishop's private archives to the general diocesan archives. And grave penalties were enacted against anyone or any group that hindered the vicar-general in this function. The punishment was a *latae sententiae* major excommunication; and if it was a chapter or a community that tried to interfere, then that chapter or community became subject to ecclesiastical interdict.[57]

The V Provincial Council of Milan (1579) included still another violation under penalty. The removal of original documents was recognized as one of the gravest of abuses, and so the bishop was empowered to inflict grave penalties for such a violation. The Council also demanded that the transgressor be made to repair any damage caused by his act of unlawful removal. If a chancellor or a notary was guilty of giving out these documents illegitimately, deprivation of office was demanded by the Council, even some additional punishment could be imposed by the bishop if he felt that it was necessary.[58]

The failure on the part of archivists and notaries to fulfill their duties evidently called for some legislation. Like the V Council of Milan (1579), the Council of Naples (1699) saw fit to warn the archivist, under penalty of formal imprisonment and of any other penalty invoked within the canonical discretion of the bishop, not to loan out any original documents.[59] Furthermore, the penalty of a *latae sententiae* excommunication was incurred by anyone who presumptuously destroyed, burned, concealed, or in any other way hid documents pertaining to the curia, the tribunal or the mensal goods or revenues of the bishop. This same penalty was invoked against anyone who at the time of the Council held any archival documents, even if legitimately obtained, but then kept them beyond a period of two months after the Council.[60]

---

[57] III Council of Milan (1573), Decr. XVIII, n. VI—Hardouin, X, 795.

[58] V Council of Milan (1579), Pars III, Const. XV—Hardouin, X, 1084.

[59] Council of Naples (1699), Tit. XII, cap. II, n. 10: "*sub poena carceris formalis aliisque ad arbitrium.*"—Coll. Lac., I, 238.

[60] Council of Naples (1699), Tit. XII, cap. II, n. 12—*Coll. Lac.*, I, 238.

In the Council of Rome (1725) the *latae sententiae* excommunication against violators who destroyed, spoiled, stole or burned documents was not re-enacted. Instead, a deprivation of authoritative station, of office, and of benefice was decreed, just as in Pius V's Constitution *Muneris Nostri* (1571). Also repeated was the fact that this deprivation extended into the future, rendering the person incapable ("*eo ipso inhabilis*") of holding any authoritative station (*dignitas*), office or benefice.[61]

The Provincial Council of Fermo (1726) was patterned after the Council of Rome (1725), and thus repeated the same penalties for violations of the law relative to archives. But one important addition in this matter was made in regard to lay persons who were guilty of the same violations. The penalty for lay persons was either a heavy fine or physical punishment. The latter punishment could entail even a condemnation to the galleys. It must be pointed out that the Archbishop of Fermo was also the Prince or civil ruler of Fermo at that period of history, and that it was in this double capacity that he could inflict a penalty which otherwise would seem unusual in ecclesiastical legislation. The conciliar law decreed that in line with their guilt lay persons were to be thus punished and that, in addition to these punishments in the external forum, a confessional absolution could not be given to these persons except with the special permission granted by the ordinary.[62]

By way of preface to the sanctions he invoked in his carefully detailed legislation for all of Italy, Benedict XIII in his Constitution *Maxima vigilantia* (1727) noted that he was enjoining its ordinances under obedience. He was imposing his laws on all ordinaries under pain of suspension of the use of the *pontificalia,* which suspension was revocable solely within the discretion of the Pontiff himself. On cathedral and collegiate chapters, the laws were imposed under penalty of interdict; on other secular clerics in Sacred Orders, under penalty of suspension *a divinis*; on regulars of either sex, under penalty both of suspension from office and also of the loss of active and passive voice in the community elections; on lay persons, under penalty of major excommunication. Absolution or dispensation from all these censures or penalties was reserved to the Roman Pontiff. This detailed section of the Constitution left no doubt of the gravity with which Pope Benedict had invested his precepts. While Pius V in his Constitution *Muneris Nostri* (1571) sought to

---

[61] Council of Rome (1725), Tit. XII, cap. V, p. 42.

[62] Council of Fermo (1726), Tit. VI—*Coll. Lac.*, I, 595.

guarantee protection for the ecclesiastical documents, Benedict XIII found it necessary to use stricter norms and penalties for the complete observance of his law.[63].

These various penalties give evidence of the constant solicitude on the part of ecclesiastical authority to preserve and protect its official documents even by invoking the use of its coercive power. Although at times the earlier enactments became abrogated through contrary custom or usage, so that also the earlier enacted penalties fell into disuse, the Church, as new needs arose, responded to the challenge with new or renewed punitive sanctions.

---

[63] Benedictus XIII, const. *Maxima vigilantia,* 14 iun. 1727, § 20—*Fontes,* n. 293.

CANONICAL COMMENTARY

CHAPTER III. ERECTION OF THE ARCHIVES

Can. 379, § 1: *Habeant praeterea Episcopi aliud archivum secretum vel saltem in communi archivo armarium seu scrinium omnino clausum et obseratum, quod de loco amoveri nequeat . . .*

Besides the general or common archives of the diocese, secret archives are expressly demanded. This obligation rests on the residential bishop. The law explicitly calls for a completely separate room, set aside purposely and exclusively for the preservation of documents of a highly secret character. But, inasmuch as the majority of the dioceses may not have so many highly secret documents as to require an entire room, the law permits the secret archives to consist in a safe or a chest in which these documents can securely be preserved. If this latter situation exists, then the safe or the chest must be kept closed and locked and must be immovable.[1]

Article I. Obligation of Erecting the Secret Archives

The obligation of erecting the diocesan secret archives becomes universal for the first time with the promulgation of the Code of Canon Law. The papal Constitution *Satis Vobis* (1741) of Benedict XIV, when treating of diocesan secret archives, simply presupposed their actual existence.[2] A later papal Constitution, *Etsi Nos* (1912) of Pius X, required secret archives for the four departments of administration of the Vicariate of Rome.[3]. These two constitutions are cited in the Code as its principal sources for the canons on diocesan secret archives, but up to the time of the Code there had been no explicit universal legislation requiring secret archives.

In speaking of the general or common archives of the diocese, Toso (+1926) unequivocally maintained that the obligation to erect archives is a matter of

[1]Augustine, *A Commentary on the New Code of Canon Law* (8 vols., Vol. II, 3 ed., St. Louis: Herder, 1919), II, 415 (hereafter cited as *Commentary;* Sipos, *Enchiridion Iuris Canonici* (Pecs [Hungary], 1926), pp. 262-263.

[2] *Supra,* p. 12.

[3] *Supra,* p. 12.

grave duty.[4] This is readily understood from the very purpose of ordinary archives, namely, the preservation of important records. *A fortiori* this would hold true if the records were especially confidential or of exceptional secrecy. D'Angelo (1885-1930) stated without hesitation that the bishop has a grave obligation, distinct from the one that requires the common or ordinary archives, to maintain separate secret archives.[5] In speaking of the ordinary diocesan archives, Cardinal Vives y Tuto (1854-1913) contended that the bishop is obliged to erect such archives "*quamprimum*".[6]

This would not necessarily be true for the secret archives. Unless there were documents on hand for the secret archives, the bishop would not be under any special urgency to erect the secret archives immediately. Surely the bishop of a newly created diocese would not be gravely obliged to erect secret archives immediately. In fact, the obligation probably would not arise until the actual need for it existed. Abstracting from this case, the Code calls for the existence of secret archives in every diocese.[7]

This obligation of erecting secret archives for the diocese rests upon the residential bishop by virtue of his pastoral office as chief shepherd and administrator of the diocese.[8] This obligation he assumes only after he has taken canonical possession of his diocese.[9] Neither his coadjutor nor his auxiliary bishops assume this obligation, unless they have been delegated by him to do so. If the coadjutor bishop has the right of succession and the residential bishop is completely incapacitated or dies or is transferred, then the coadjutor becomes the residential bishop. In such a case, if the previous residential bishop has neglected to erect secret archives, the successor inherits the obliga-

---

[4] "*Et primum hoc in canone* (*can.* 375) *fit Ordinariis praeceptum grave de archivo constituendo . . .*"—Toso, *Ad Codicem Iuris Canonici Commentaria Minora* (5 vols. in 2, Vol. IV [Lib. II, *De Personis,* Pars I, Tomus III], Romae:Ius Pontificium, 1925), IV. 22.

[5] *La curia Diocesana a norma del Codice di Diritto Canonico* (Giarre, Sicilia: Pietro Lisi, 1922), p. 110 (hereafter cited as D'Angelo).

[6] *De Dignitate et Officiis Episcoporum et Praelatorum* (Romae: Pustet, 1905), p. 215, n. 1551 (hereafter cited as Vives y Tuto).

[7] "*Ergo primo universaliter imponitur Episcopis obligatio habendi separatim secretum archivium, aut saltem in communi tabulario armarium seu scrinium . . .*"—Wernz-Vidal, II, p. 819, n. 648, art. I; Coronata, *Institutiones Iuris Canonici* (5 vols., Vols. I, II, 4. ed., Taurini: Marietti, 1950-1951), Vol. I, 498-500 (hereafter cited as Coronata).

[8] Can. 335, § 1.

[9] Can. 334, § 2.

tion. An auxiliary bishop would not inherit the obligation unless he were to succeed to the government of the diocese as residential bishop.

Should the diocese become vacant or quasi-vacant, the obligation could devolve upon the cleric who assumes the government of the diocese.[10] However, since such a person would take over the government of the diocese only temporarily, it is unlikely that the obligation of erecting secret archives would be grave for him. Rather, it would be more prudent to postpone this function until the new residential bishop has been installed.

Once the residential bishop has taken canonical possession of the diocese, he is responsible for its government and is the custodian of ecclesiastical discipline. The existence of the secret archives pertains to his executive or administrative activity. Paragraph 1 of canon 335 states the general principle that bishops have the right and duty to govern their diocese in accordance with the norms of the sacred canons. Therefore in the administration of his diocese, the bishop's executive authority is directed to the immediate practical application of all the laws, universal and particular, which are in force in his diocese.[11] Consequently, the good administration of his diocese requires the bishop to fulfill as soon as possible and as well as possible this explicit obligation placed on him by virtue of canon 379, § 1.

Article II. Construction of the Secret Archives

The site for the erection of the secret archives will depend upon circumstances in the diocese and particularly in the curia. Generally the curia or chancery building is the most logical and feasible location. If sufficient room or adequate facilities are not available, the bishop may choose some other diocesan building which is accessible, or he may prefer to house the archives, including the secret archives, in the episcopal residence.[12]

The Council of Toledo (1565) urged the bishops to erect their archives in a monastery.[13] The Plenary Council of Thurles (1850) simply required each

---

[10] A see is said to be quasi-vacant when its residential bishop is prevented from exercising his jurisdiction in person. Abbo-Hannan, *The Sacred Canons* (2 vols., St. Louis: Herder, 1952), I, 428.

[11] Ryan, *Principles of Episcopal Jurisdiction,* the Catholic University of America Canon Law Studies, n. 120 (Washington, D. C., The Catholic Universiity of America Press, 1939), p. 141.

[12] Vives y Tuto, p. 228, n. 1649.

[13] *Supra,* p. 13.

of the Irish dioceses to have its archives in a very safe and convenient place.[14] The Code makes no recommendations whatsoever, but by placing the responsibility for these secret archives entirely in the hands of the bishop the determination of a particular site is concomitantly left to the discretion of the bishop.

In the construction of the secret archives there rarely would be any question of a large room or vault. The number of highly secret documents in the average diocese would hardly be more than a drawerful. However, the canon does insist that the secret archives be entirely closed and locked, and that they be immovable. Therefore a desk drawer or a filing cabinet, howsoever locked, would be inadequate because neither would be sufficiently immovable. Augustine (1872-1943) pointed to a safe or a safety vault as meeting the requirements.[15] Hence a safe within a vault, or a smaller, although immovable, safe within the general archives would suffice.

According to canon 379, § 3, the secret archives must be so constructed and locked that they can be opened only through the use of two different keys. If combination locks are used instead of keys, the combinations must differ.

The danger of burglary of the chancery archives, whether of the general or the secret archives, is ordinarily remote. Chanceries are seldom known to house any financial amount which would attract burglars. Therefore, the need of extreme protection against burglary is rarely existent. But that does not mean that prudent precautions are to be neglected. The obligation of custody will be discussed shortly, but here it may well be noted that the Code demands that the contents of the secret archives be guarded most carefully. The use of the superlative clearly indicates the grave responsibility to protect and preserve the documents consigned to the secret archives. Therefore an old or obsolete type of safe which can be opened with ordinary burglary tools and equipment would not be adequate.

The two keys prescribed by the Code would be of little protection if the archives safe or vault would be deficient in any way in its design or construction. As it has been pointed out, extreme protection in the form of elaborate and massive vaults is not necessary, for even the smaller safes are dependable and adequate. A curia with a fifty-year old safe should have that safe inspected. Physical deterioration in the walls and doors and especially in the

---

[14] *Supra*, p. 15.

[15] *Commentary*, II, 415.

locks could have ensued. Combination locks in particular should be serviced, and the combination itself should be changed periodically.[16] Unless the safes or vaults are subjected to constant use, most curias would probably find biennial servicing sufficient.

The danger of fire is always present, even in fireproof buildings. The fire hazard is dependent upon two things: the duration and the intensity of the fire. Non-fireproof buildings usually provide fires of longer duration. Fireproof buildings usually provide fires of greater intensity, inasmuch as a fireproof building, like an oven, retains and intensifies the heat of the fire. If, therefore, a fire breaks out in the curia building or in that part of the building which houses the archives, the archives vault or safe may be of doubtful protective value.

Old safes have ordinary concrete walls which dry out and crack over the years or because of a fire. Also the door fit in these old safes may be such that heat could enter the safe. In both cases the passage of heat into the safe could char the records and documents within. The cast-iron jambs of the old safes not only conduct heat into the safe but also could shatter under impact. Furthermore, the old safes could generate gases which often causes them to explode in fires.

A recognized authority on archives writes: "The chief danger in fact is not lest the building itself, in such a case, should catch fire or suffer from damp, but lest neighboring buildings should catch fire and by their collapse, by flying fragments of flaming material, by the mere heat generated in their burning, or by the water poured in to save them, damage the repository or its contents."[17] In the light of these dangers, it is incumbent upon the residential bishop as part of his pastoral office to give careful attention to the adequate protection of important documents in his diocesan secret archives.[18]

---

[16] The majority of big business firms have their safes and vaults serviced annually.

[17] Jenkinson, *A Manual of Archive Administration* (Oxford: The Clarendon Press, 1922), p. 45.

[18] Modern safes of most safe manufacturers are certified by two organizations. The Underwriters' Laboratories, Inc., an independent testing organization, specifies the minimum certified protection that the safe will provide, e. g., some safes are capable of withstanding severe fire for four hours at temperatures reaching 2000° Fahrenheit before the interior of the safe reaches 350° Fahrenheit, and also withstand concentrated burglarious attack by drills, sledge hammers, wedges and mechanical tools for twenty minutes.

The building and the room housing the archives must have the normal protections against burglary, fire and other dangers. The construction of the building must be in keeping with the important function of the building as the depository of highly confidential material. Surely the room for the general or common archives must be safe and suitable.[19] And the secret archives, either as a separate room or as a safe in the general archives, must be such as to guarantee complete protection to the contents therein.

The need for precautions in general against theft and fire has already been stressed. These precautions, as a rule, afford adequate protection for the secret archives themselves as long as attention has been given primarily to the building and that section of the building wherein the secret archives are kept. The requirements relative to the construction of the safe or vault for the secret archives, as well as the requirements relative to the two canonical keys, will afford the additional safeguards called for on the part of the secret archives.

The Safe Manufacturers National Association conducts similar independent tests to meet exacting fire-resistance and impact specifications. These warranties are accepted by insurance companies without question for pertinent rate discounts.

[19] Louis, p. 44.

CHAPTER IV. CONTENTS OF THE SECRET ARCHIVES

Can. 379, § 1—. . . *In eo scripturae secreto servandae cautissime custodiantur*; . . .

The Code demands that those writings which must be preserved secretly are to be guarded most carefully in the secret archives. But the Code purposely avoids giving a comprehensive list of the matters and documents that must be committed to the secret archives. In various canons, the Code explicitly commands that certain documentary evidence be preserved in the secret archives. Other confidential matters, while not specifically mentioned, likewise seem to be included in the tenor of the law. Therefore with a view to a better grasp of the purpose of the law, this dissertation will consider the content material of the secret archives according to the nature of the documents. Accordingly, the articles to be preserved in the secret archives will receive their specific determination not only in the light of the Code requirements but also from the fact that they constitute kindred matters which the ordinary may, according to circumstances, likewise preserve in his diocesan secret archives.

Article 1. Material Pertaining to Matrimony

Throughout its remarkable history the Church has shown the greatest solicitude in protecting the dignity and sanctity of the sacrament of matrimony. Obedient to the will of its Founder, the Church has made every effort to make the reception of this sacrament, as well as of the others, always possible to worthy persons. Realizing that circumstances can occur which would prevent its subjects from receiving the sacrament of matrimony in the ordinary manner, the Church has sought to give them every opportunity to receive this sacrament even in special, extraordinary cases.

By means of two canonical institutes, the Church permits marriages that involve secrecy, and in both institutes uses the secret archives for the custody and protection of the records of these exceptional cases. These two institutes concern dispensations from occult impediments.[20] and marriages of conscience.[21]

[20] Can. 1047.

[21] Canons 1104-1107.

Section 1. Dispensation from Occult Impediments

Can. 1047—*Nisi aliud ferat S. Poenitentiariae rescriptum, dispensatio in foro interno non sacramentali concessa super impedimento occulto, adnotetur in libro diligenter in secreto Curiae archivo de quo in can. 379 asservando, nec alia dispensatio pro foro externo est necessaria, si dispensatio concessa fuerat tantum in foro interno sacramentali.*

Dispensations from matrimonial impediments may be given in the external or in the internal forum. There is exclusive concern here with certain dispensations granted for the internal forum. Furthermore, the consideration will deal only with the non-sacramental internal forum. While the same dispensations may be obtained in the sacramental internal forum, such dispensations would involve a special procedure which would not pertain to the secret archives of the diocese. For dispensations in the internal forum, sacramental or non-sacramental, the Roman Pontiff generally uses the Sacred Penitentiary for all occult impediments and for all persons, including Orientals.[22]

Finally, the discussion here will deal only with occult impediments, and therefore no thought will be given to public impediments. Canon 1037 reads: "An impediment is said to be public, when it can be proved in the external forum, otherwise it is occult." This canon is of great importance and warrants some explanation. "*Publicum censetur impedimentum*" implies that even if the impediment is in fact occult, as long as there is a possibility of proof it must be considered public. When this possibility of proof is wanting, the impediment is occult.[23]

The penal section of the Code speaks of a crime as *materially occult* when there is secret the act of the crime itself, and *formally occult* when its imputability is hidden.[24] But this distinction is not made in reference to impediments. An impediment is said (*censetur*) to be occult when it cannot be proved in the external forum.[25]

---

[22] S. C. Orient., 10 mail, 1930—*AAS*, XXII (1930), 394; Cf. Bouscaren, *Canon Law Digest* (2 vols., and Supplement through 1948, Milwaukee: Bruce Publishing Co., Vol. I, 1934; Vol. II, 1943; Supplement, 1949), I, 174 (hereafter cited as Bouscaren).

[23] Gougnard, *Tractatus de Matrimonio* (7. ed., Mechliniae: Dessain, 1931), p. 483 (hereafter cited as Gougnard).

[24] Can. 2197, § 4.

[25] Kubelbeck, *The Sacred Penitentiaria and its Relations to Faculties of Ordinaries and*

Furthermore, the Code Commission has declared that, to constitute an impediment as public it suffices that the fact from which it arises is public.[26] Hence, as Bouscaren points out, the distinction between materially and formally public is now of relatively slight consequence in speaking of impediments.[27] Therefore, when canon 1047 speaks of occult impediments it means those impediments which lack proof through documents or witnesses.[28] And yet the Sacred Penitentiary will at times dispense from an impediment which is not occult in the sense of canon 1037, but which is known only to a few discreet persons, if it can be presumed that there is no danger of its becoming generally known.[29]

Ordinarily there are only three entirely occult impediments that yield to dispensation: the impediment of private simple vows (canon 1058), the impediment of crime (canon 1075), and the impediment of consanguinity when it derives through illicit intercourse (canon 1076).[30]

It suffices to mention here that the following are competent to grant dispensations from these occult impediments: the Sacred Penitentiary, the local ordinary, the pastor, the priest mentioned in canon 1098, § 2, and the confessor. The Sacred Penitentiary is the tribunal that deals exclusively with matters of the internal forum, and as one of the departments of the Roman Curia it acts with ordinary jurisdiction.[31]

The ordinary of the place may grant dispensations in virtue of ordinary or extraordinary concessions of the common law, or in consequence of delegated

---

Priests, The Catholic University of America Canon Law Studies, n. 5 (Washington, D. C.: The Catholic University of America, 1918), p. 46 (hereafter cited as Kubelbeck); Gougnard, p. 483; Wernz-Vidal, V, n. 147.

[26] Pont. Comm. Intr., 25 iun. 1932—*AAS,* XXIV (1932), 284; Cf. Bouscaren, *Digest,* I, 501.

[27] Bouscaren-Ellis, *Canon Law* (2. ed., Milwaukee: Bruce Publishing Co., 1952), p. 431.

[28] For the question regarding canonical proof, cf. can. 1747.

[29] Cf. Chelodi-Ciprotti, *Ius Canonicum De Matrimonio* (5. ed. by Ciprotti, Vicenza (Italy): Società Anomina Tipografica Editrice, 1947), p. 42 (hereafter cited as Chelodi-Ciprotti); Gougnard, p. 483.

[30] It seems called for to say "ordinarily," for it is conceivable that no adequate proof could be presented for the birth date of a child born out of wedlock in a small, rural community. Likewise, a previous marriage bond may lack any proof, for it could exist as a valid common law marriage, or the marriage records may have been destroyed, e. g., in warfare or in a fire, and no witnesses to the marriage are living.

[31] Cf. can. 258; Kubelbeck, pp. 35-42.

faculties.[82] The pastor likewise receives ordinary powers from the common law, as does any priest when he acts within the situation contemplated in canon 1098, § 2. The confessor receives the same power of dispensing as the pastor, except that he may act only in the sacramental forum, in which case no record is kept, and therefore the confessor's function does not concern the present discussion of the contents of the secret archives.[83]

When, as explained, a dispensation from an occult impediment is obtained, canon 1047 requires that a record be kept of the granting of this dispensation. Unless the Sacred Penitentiary determines that the record be kept in its own secret archives, the record must be preservd in the diocesan secret archives. The Code is even more explicit; it demands that such records be annotated in a special book for this purpose. Therefore loose documents or papers regarding such dispensations are not in accordance with the common law.

The records of dispensations granted from occult impediments and for the internal non-sacramental forum must be kept in a book provided for the containing of such information. And this book must be kept in the secret archives. Furthermore, the prescriptions of canon 379, § 1, regarding the burning of documents retained in the secret archives certainly do not pertain to the records of dispensations from occult impediments. Only those documents must be burned which concern criminal cases, as will be seen later.

Section 2. Marriages of Conscience

Can 1107—*Matrimonium conscientiae non est adnotandum in consueto matrimoniorum ac baptizatorium libro, sed in peculiari libro servando in secreto Curiae archivo de quo in can. 379.*

In the canonical institute known as the marriage of conscience, the Church has provided legislation which touches such cases wherein marriage and secrecy are both necessary as contrasted to the usual public marriage.[84]

---

[82] Regarding ordinary power of dispensing, cf. especially canons 1043 and 1045; regarding delegated faculties, cf. Eagleton, *The Diocesan Quinquennial Faculties, Formula IV,* The Catholic University of America Canon Law Studies, n. 248 (Washington, D. C.: The Catholic University of America Press, 1948), pp. 70-85 (hereafter cited as Eagleton).

[83] Cf. canons 1044 and 1045.

[84] For a thorough and careful study of this subject, cf. Coburn, *Marriages of Conscience,* The Catholic University of America Canon Law Studies, n. 191 (Washington, D. C.: The Catholic University of America Press, 1944) (hereafter cited as Coburn); also Ayrinhac-Lydon, pp. 281-285.

A marriage of conscience is one which is celebrated in the form prescribed by law, but in such a manner that it may remain a secret and unknown among the people. The law prohibits the publication of the banns and demands that the secrecy be observed by the local ordinary, by the priest who assists at the marriage, by the parties themselves and also by the witnesses to the marriage. After the marriage a record of it must be sent to the local ordinary to be retained in the secret archives of the diocese.

It may be helpful to point out that not all marriages unknown to the public or celebrated with attempts to maintain secrecy are marriages of conscience. The concept of this canonical institute is precisely and carefully detailed in four canons of the Code.[35]

The registration of these marriages may not be entered in the ordinary marriage and baptismal registers.[36] The Code prescribes special books to be kept in the secret archives of the diocese for these records. Separate documents or even folders would not meet the requirements of the law. Coburn rightly insists that the manner of preserving the records pertaining to marriages of conscience in the secret archives is not optional, but prescribed by law.[37]

Furthermore, since it is the common practice to keep the records of marriages and baptisms in separate books, it seems more logical and preferable to have separate books in the secret archives, one for the recording of the marriages of conscience, and the other for the records of the subsequent baptisms.

Ordinarily the registration of marriages includes all the essential information. The registration of the marriages of conscience should do the same, giving the full names of the parties, the witnesses, the priest assisting and the place, as also the date of the marriage. Mention of the granting of any dispensations must be included, except the one from the banns, since such a dispensation is implied and contained in the permission given by the local ordinary for the celebration of the marriage in question.[38]

If the local ordinary wishes to preserve, in addition to the records fully transcribed in the books of the secret archives, any or all of the documents

---

[35] Canons 1104-1107.

[36] Coburn, p. 123; Wernz-Vidal, V, n. 570.

[37] *Marriages of Conscience*, p. 124.

[38] Coburn, p. 85.

pertaining to each case, he may keep these in a separate file. Actually, there is almost no advantage in such a procedure, and it would simply multiply records of the same facts in the same place. If the registration in the secret archives books is complete there will be no need of any other documents. Marginal notations could take care of any pertinent facts beyond the primary legal proofs contained in the registers.

Regarding copies of records from these registers of marriages and baptisms, the local ordinary as the custodian of the secret archives is the authority to decide whether the requested copy is to be issued. Wernz-Vidal cite the need for the administration of justice as a general norm to govern the issuance of copies of the record.[39] Thus, use of these records as essential proofs in ecclesiastical tribunals would be a sufficient reason to issue a copy. In a footnote, Wernz-Vidal maintain that use of these records in the civil courts would not be a sufficient reason to permit the bishop to issue copies of marriage of conscience records from the secret archives. The danger of violating grave secrecy is too imminent.[40]

On the other hand, the issuance of baptismal records from the secret archives is more easily possible. Again, the local ordinary is the sole authority to decide when and in what manner such information may be supplied. If the baptismal record pertains to a child of a marriage of conscience union and this marriage of conscience must remain a secret, the local ordinary may decide to issue the record merely of the fact of baptism without any reference to the names of the parents. This could easily obtain if the child is about to be confirmed and needs the baptismal record to prove Catholicity upon registering for school. Or the local ordinary, in issuing the record, may use assumed names if the record was originally inscribed in that manner in the parish register.

In the issuing of a baptismal record from the secret archives so that the person involved may present it as a proof of Catholicity on the occasion of marriage, special precautions will very likely be necessary. If the marriage of conscience of the parents is still a secret and therefore the parentage of the prospective bride or groom is not known to the public, the local ordinary ought to intervene in the prenuptial investigation in order to insure the valid and lawful celebration of marriage.

---

[39] Wernz-Vidal, V, n. 570.

[40] Wernz-Vidal, V, n. 570.

A simple testimony from the local ordinary that the person involved was baptized would suffice for the pastor, and the local ordinary could include the date of baptism, the names of the sponsors and of the minister of baptism. After the pastor has completed the prenuptial investigation as completely as possible, the local ordinary should demand that the interrogatories be sent to him for study. Then he would be able to determine from a comparison of the interrogatories and his secret archives material whether there are any obstacles to the marriage. Thus consanguinity and affinity could be checked much more carefully, as also any possibility of spiritual or legal relationship.

If, in the course of time, a marriage of conscience is divulged, it should be recorded in the ordinary marriage register of the parish. This recording should be made in the register of the parish in which the marriage actually took place. If the local ordinary, in order to guarantee the secrecy of the marriage, permitted it to be celebrated outside of a church,[41] then he could now require the public recording of the marriage to be in the register of the parish in which the marriage would have taken place under ordinary circumstances. Or, if this would not be feasible, then it could be recorded in the register of the parish in which the private home, the chancery, or whatever the place of marriage, was actually located. Finally, the local ordinary could, because of special circumstances, permit the public recording to be in the register of the present domicile or quasi-domicile of the parties.

This public recording of the marriage must be made at the command of the local ordinary, since he is responsible for the existence of a record in the secret archives if necessary, and in the public register if the secrecy is no longer necessary. And the public recording must take place whether the fact of the secret marriage of conscience has been made public by the decision of the bishop or of the parties, and even if the publicity is due to the culpable imprudence of others.[42] Once the marriage of conscience has been brought out of the forum of conscience and into the external forum, it should conform to the norms of the external forum, particularly in whatever pertains to the probative value of these records in the ordinary regimen of the Church.

---

[41] Coburn suggests as suitable places in such circumstances a private home, the chancery office, the rectory of the parish where the parties live, or a Catholic hospital.

[42] Cappello, *Tractatus Canonico-Moralis de Sacramentis,* 5 vols., Vol. V, *De Matrimonio,* 6. ed., Taurini-Romae: Marietti, (1950), p. 709, n. 724 (hereafter cited as *De Sacramentis*) ; Coburn, p. 128.

In the recording of public marriages, notice of the fact of the marriage in each case is to be entered in the baptismal register where the baptism of the parties was originally recorded[43] But such notations are not to be made when the marriage is a marriage of conscience, nor are notices to be sent, for such action would endanger the essential secrecy of the marriage. Later, if and when the marriage of conscience is divulged, it should be recorded in the proper baptismal register.

In the same way, the individual baptismal record kept in the secret archives should, when the marriage of conscience of the parents is divulged, be transferred to the ordinary parochial register of baptism.

For the transcription of these marriage and baptismal records from the secret archives to the parochial registers, Wernz-Vidal make a very practical and logical observation. They suggest that this transcription be placed immediately after the last recorded marriage or baptism, and that a notation be made in the book at the place where the record would have been inserted if the marriage had not been celebrated secretly.[44]

After this transcription has been made, there is no need of removing the record from the special book of the secret archives. The book should be left intact; it should not be soiled or disfigured with erasures or blottings. Since the record has been placed in the public registers, there is no harm or defamation that can come from its continued existence in this secret register, which is always under such strict custody, although a notation of the transfer should be made in the margin.

Other documents pertinent to the case which the local ordinary had decided to keep in the secret archives should now be removed. In the absence of any potential utility they should be destroyed, and otherwise they should be kept in the parish archives where the marriage is registered. That these documents should be transferred when the marriage of conscience is divulged is evident from the nature of the secret archives, namely their purpose of safeguarding highly secret and confidential matter. Therefore the local ordinary should make every effort to keep the secret archives free of materials and documents that have no rightful existence in this specialized depository. On the other hand, if the local ordinary feels that the good administration of his

---

[43] Canons 1103, § 2, and 470, § 2.

[44] Wernz-Vidal, V, n. 570.

diocese determines that these records should continue to be preserved in the secret archives he can, as befits his pastoral office, leave them in the secret archives.

A final word ought to be mentioned about the actual decree from the Sacred Penitentiary or from the local ordinary who granted permission for the celebration of the marriage of conscience. Cappello says that this decree should be preserved in the proper parochial archives.[45] But this would surely seem to endanger the necessary secrecy of marriage. And therefore Coburn more correctly maintains that it appears to reflect a more uniform and safe method if all the records relating to these marriages were preserved in the secret archives.[46]

Thus, in a brief consideration of these two canonical institutes pertaining to matrimony, one sees the part played by the secret archives in protecting exceptional cases involving secrecy. Should the local ordinary be faced with matrimonial cases which demand somewhat similar arrangements, the two procedures here discussed can serve as patterns, since the Code itself does not discuss any other matrimonial situations which would demand the use of the secret archives.[47]

Section 3. Additional Material

O'Rourke notes the possibility of using the secret archives for the recording of some marriages visualized in canon 1098 with a view to saving the fame of the person concerned and yet with the effect of furnishing available proof of the legitimacy of the children.[48] He likewise points to the secret archives for the recording of a marriage known as the *matrimonium iureiurando probatum,* that is, when persons unable to show legitimate proof of their contracting of marriage in some distant place are accepted upon their oath as legitimately married, and their children as of legitimate status.[49] And lastly, convalidations of marriages granted for the internal non-sacramental forum

---

[45] *De Sacramentis,* Vol. V, n. 289 bis.

[46] *Marriages of Conscience,* p. 134.

[47] Can. 20.

[48] *Parish Registers,* The Catholic University of America Canon Law Studies, n. 88 (Washington, D. C.: The Catholic University of America, 1934), p. 73 (hereafter cited as O'Rourke).

[49] *Ibidem,* p. 74.

should, he remarks, be registered in the secret archives as a precaution against a future divulging which would involve the legitimacy of the children.[50]

De facto, convalidations will rarely demand such secrecy, and generally the recording in the ordinary register will suffice.

Article II. Material Pertaining to Clerics

By divine institution, individuals were chosen to exercise among the faithful the sacred ministry in the Church. These individuals from the earliest times were called clerics. The word is derived from the Greek word *kleros,* meaning "lot," "portion," "heritage."[51] In general, then, clerics are those members of the Church who occupy positions of preeminence by reason either of the power of orders or of the power of jurisdiction.

The Church has always exercised the greatest solicitude for the members of the clergy. This could not be otherwise, since the well-being of the entire Church will depend greatly upon the uprightness, zeal and sanctity of those who are set aside as leaders and ministers in the Church.

In this dissertation one sees this solicitude manifested in the protection and care shown toward those clerics who may be the victims of delinquencies or may themselves be delinquents. The concern of the Church is both for the good of the Church itself as well as the good of the individual clerics.

Can. 991, § 4—*Dispensatio [ab irregularitatibus et impedimentis], in foro interno non sacramentali concessa, scripto consignetur; et de ea in secreto Curiae libro constare debet.*

Since the priest is to be another Christ, it is fitting not only that worthy candidates be admitted to the ministry, but in addition that these candidates be capable of performing their duties with that decency and decorum which the sacred character of such duties and the Church require. Consequently, the Church has determined that certain defects and crimes constitute an obstacle to Holy Orders. These obstacles are called irregularities and impediments. The Church can dispense individuals from these obstacles whenever they are so

---

[50] *Ibidem,* p. 76.

[51] S. Hieronymus, *Ep.* LII: *"Propterea vocantur clerici vel quia de sorte sunt Domini, vel quia ipse Dominus sors, idest, pars clericorum est."*—*MPL,* XXII, 531.

constituted by ecclesiastical legislation, but *de facto* in some cases the Church does so only rarely, and in some species it never dispenses.[52]

The nature and species of these disqualifications are set forth in the Code in seven canons.[53] Two additional canons govern the dispensations available in regard to them.[54] Here the question turns solely about those dispensations which are granted for the internal non-sacramental forum. Dispensations of this kind will ordinarily be given very rarely, but if and when they are thus given the Church desires to safeguard the lawfulness and the validity of Holy Orders.

The Roman Pontiff is, of course, the primary source of dispensations from all irregularities, but he generally acts through his curia. For dispensations from public irregularities he generally uses the agency either of the Sacred Congregation of the Sacraments, or of the Sacred Congregation for Religious, or also of other Congregations when the rule regarding competence so demands it. For dispensations in the internal forum for occult irregularities, the Holy Father generally uses the Sacred Penitentiary.[55]

Direct recourse to the Sacred Penitentiary is not so necessary as one might suppose, inasmuch as ordinaries have ample powers, either ordinary or delegated, to deal with the cases which frequently occur.

Local ordinaries may dispense their subjects, first of all, from all doubtful irregularities, if it is a question of a *dubium facti,* provided that the case is such that the Holy See usually grants the dispensation; if it is a question of a *dubium iuris,* the law would not bind, and therefore no dispensation would be necessary.[56] Furthermore, local ordinaries may dispense from all irregularities arising from an occult delict, with the exception of the irregularity incurred through voluntary homicide or abortion, and of any other irregularity

---

[52] Cf. Hickey, *Irregularities and Simple Impediments,* The Catholic University of America Canon Law Studies, n. 7 (Washington, D. C.: The Catholic University of America, 1920), pp. 86-93 (hereafter cited as Hickey).

[53] Liber III, Tit. VI, Cap. II, Art. II, canones 983-989.

[54] *Ibidem,* canones 990-991.

[55] Cf. Hickey, p. 86; Cappello, *Summa Iuris Canonici* (3 vols., Vol. II, 4. ed. Romae: Apud Aedes Universitatis Gregorianae, 1945), II, p. 270, n. 279 (hereafter cited as *Summa*); Ramstein, *Manual of Canon Law* (2. ed. rev., Hoboken, N. J.: Terminal Printing & Publishing Co., 1948), p. 213.

[56] Can. 15.

regarding which cognizance has been taken in a judicial forum. The purpose of this concession of the law is the avoidance of scandal. If the delict is known to only a few persons who can be relied upon not to reveal it, it remains occult. However, if the delict is known publicly, the ordinary is not empowered to grant a dispensation even if the irregularity as such is occult.[57]

By virtue of the quinquennial faculties, the ordinary is now delegated to dispense from the irregularity incurred because of voluntary homicide or abortion.[58] But this delegated faculty may be used only on behalf of those who are clerics and who are either the perpetrators of, or active accomplices in, the two above mentioned delicts. In addition, the only reason for the valid use of this faculty consists in the purpose that the cleric may exercise the Orders already received, and that only by exercising these Orders will the cleric escape infamy for himself and obviate the danger of scandal for others.[59]

Confessors who are regulars may by privilege dispense all penitents from those irregularities from which by common law the local ordinary can dispense. Therefore regular confessors enjoy the faculties granted in canons 15 and 990, § 1, to ordinaries.

Other confessors enjoy the same faculties as granted to the local ordinary in canon 990, § 1, but only in very urgent, occult cases, when the delinquent is not able to approach the ordinary in person either by letter or by agent and there is imminent danger of grave loss (material or spiritual). Furthermore, confessors may use this faculty only in order to permit a cleric to exercise his Orders, and never for advancement to Orders.[60] The confessor can exercise

---

[57] Can. 990, § 1, and 2237, § 2; Abbo-Hannan, II, 141.

[58] Bouscaren, *Digest,* II, p. 40, n. 9; Eagleton, pp. 168-170.

[59] "*Dispensandi ab irregularitate ex homicidio voluntario aut abortu, de qua in can.* 985, 4°, *sed ad hoc dumtaxat ut poenitens ordines iam susceptos sine infamiae vel scandali periculo exercere queat; iniuncto eidem poenitenti onere intra mensem, saltem per epistolam, per alium vel per se, reticito nomine, docendi de omnibus casus circumstantiis, et praesertim quoties delictum patraverit, ad S. P. recurrendi et standi eius mandatis sub poena suspensionis a divinis ipso facto incurrendae.*"—Art. 9, Faculties from the Sacred Penitentiary. Cf. Pius XI, motu propr. *Post datam,* 20 apr. 1923—*AAS,* XV (1923), 193-194.

[60] Cappello, however, believes that the confessor could dispense in order to permit advancement to Orders if the irregularity is dubious with regard to the very fact of its existence; the granting of such a dispensation, he says, would be subject to the usual

this power even outside the confessional, but only over those whose confession he *de facto* has the jurisdiction to hear.[61]

When a dispensation is granted by any of the above mentioned competent individuals for the internal sacramental forum, no record of the dispensation may be kept. If the dispensation is granted for the internal non-sacramental forum, a record must be kept in the secret archives of the curia.[62] If this record must be kept secret even from the local ordinary, then the record must be preserved in the secret archives of the Sacred Penitentiary.

Cappello remarks that this annotation in the secret archives may become exceedingly burdensome or almost impossible, and therefore he believes that in such cases it may be omitted, or the dispensation should be given in the sacramental forum.[63] However, such cases would be most exceptional, and the existence of secret archives in either the diocesan curia or the Sacred Penitentiary indicates the desire on the part of the Church to have a record of such granted dispensations.

The safeguards for the good reputation of the individual are guaranteed through the careful prescriptions given in law for the secret archives. The dignity of Holy Orders is protected from unnecessary doubts concerning their valid or lawful reception or use in view of the existence of a record of any dispensations granted. The local ordinary is able to comprehend not only the ordinary but also the exceptional situations in his diocese. It will help him to administer his diocese more confidently as also more advantageously if he is aware of even the unusual circumstances connected with his clergy and faithful.

Since canon 991, § 4, prescribes that evidence of these dispensations from irregularities be recorded in a secret register of the curia, the manner of preserving these records is not optional. Therefore, merely placing the original document of dispensation in the secret archives would not meet the requirements of the law. After the record has been transcribed in the secret book,

---

conditions: the ordinary cannot be reached, voluntary homicide and abortion are excepted, and recourse to the ordinary or to the Sacred Penitentiary must be imposed.—*Summa,* II, 271.

[61] Beste, *Introductio in Codicem* (3. ed., Collegeville, Minn.: St. John's Abbey Press, 1946), p. 542.

[62] Can. 991, § 4.

[63] *Summa,* II, 272.

the original document must be destroyed if the very purpose of the law is to obtain its effect. The single record in the secret register will suffice for the needs of the Church.

It is usually required that the confessor (or the executor) shall burn the rescript within three days, but this does not prevent his retaining a copy of it for his own guidance.[64] It seems, however, that prudence will demand that, if the name of the dispensed individual is mentioned in the rescript, the confessor's copy should omit this name.

If proof is ever needed for the external forum, the local ordinary alone has the right and the duty to make use of the secret information, as he prudently sees fit. The secret register can have probative value even in the external forum, but the local ordinary as custodian of the secret archives is free to withhold any release of such confidential material. In other words, information from this secret register need not be dragged into the external forum at every request. The good of the individual as well as the good of the Church will guide the local ordinary in his judgment concerning the publicizing of any information from the secret archives. He might even prefer to grant a new dispensation for the external forum, without any reference to what may have been done in the internal forum.

When a dispensation for the internal forum from an occult irregularity is received from the Sacred Penitentiary, then the executor of the rescript, if he be the local ordinary, shall after the execution of the rescript take care that the transcription is made into the special book of the secret archives. If a priest applied to the Sacred Penitentiary for a dispensation for an individual, that priest must then send all the information to the local ordinary for the recording in the secret archives. Actually, the priest should have consulted the ordinary before requesting the dispensation from the Sacred Penitentiary, in order that the ordinary could include his own recommendation (*votum*) in forwarding the request to the Sacred Penitentiary.[65]

When the petition is sent through the ordinary, the answer from the Sacred Penitentiary will generally be addressed to that ordinary. Hickey believes that the recommendation should be made by the ordinary who is to confer the

---

[64] Abbo-Hannan, I, 314.

[65] Cf. Kubelbeck, p. 86; Hickey, p. 89.

Orders.[66] This will not always be true, however, since it is not always the proper ordinary according to canon 955 who will confer the Orders. Therefore it would be more correct to say that the recommendation should be given by the proper ordinary, whether the Orders are conferred on a candidate to the secular or the religious priesthood, and whether the Orders are conferred in virtue of granted dismissorials or in consequence of an already possessed prerogative in law.

If the local ordinary granted the dispensation from irregularities, then he himself must complete the process by recording the fact in the secret archives. If the request had come to him from a priest on behalf of an individual, then in notifying the priest of the granted dispensation, the bishop should inform him that a record of the dispensation has been entered in the secret archives. In that way all concerned will be aware of the record in case of any future questions.

If a confessor, whether a regular or otherwise, granted the dispensation according to the faculties cited above, he should send information of this to the local ordinary with a request that a record of it be entered in the secret archives. This is done, however, only if the dispensation was granted in the non-sacramental forum.

Article III. Material Pertaining to Criminal Cases

It seems significant that the only kind of documents specifically mentioned in canon 379, § 1, concerning the contents of the secret archives are the documents that pertain to criminal processes which deal with matters of morality. The prevailing intention of the legislator in prescribing secret archives is manifest in this reference to criminal matters; the constant concern for the rights of defendants as well as for the prevention of any miscarriage of justice prompts the Church to demand every safeguard possible.

Whether one looks to judicial trials or to extrajudicial procedures, one finds the Church exercising its coercive power with moderation and restraint. Thus, in the penal section of the Code, the legislator renews the admonitions of the Council of Trent[67] that ordinaries should have recourse to penal measures only

---

[66] Hickey, p. 89.
[67] Sess. XIII, *de ref.*, c. 1.

when persuasion or reproaches have failed, and even then they should proceed with mercy, benevolence, without harshness or undue rigor.[68]

In order to appreciate the function of the diocesan secret archives in criminal matters, one must look to judicial trials and then to extrajudicial procedures and note the prescribed or implied use of the secret archives for the documents in both procedures.

Section 1. Judicial Trials

When a law or a precept has been violated, either a criminal or a contentious suit may be introduced in court. A criminal trial is one which seeks to ascertain whether the law was violated, and, if so, to apply the penalty decreed for the violation.[69] A contentious trial seeks the prosecution or vindication of rights, or the declaration of a juridical fact.[70] Contentious trials will seldom require the use of the secret archives of the diocese as a depository for its *acta.* If a contentious case should warrant such a use, then the proceedings as set forth for criminal cases can serve as a pattern according to the general principle of canon 20.

Before any criminal action at court can be undertaken, the essential and fundamental object postulated by law, namely the existence of a public crime,[71] must actually be verified. In all cases wherein the crime is not yet fully certified, or in which an admission or confession of guilt has not intervened, a previous special investigation must be made if the way is to be prepared for a formal accusation in court, which eventually will be followed by the court's judicial sentence. Eight canons of the Code outline this procedure known as the *inquisitio specialis.*[72]

In brief, such an investigation to determine whether and how far the incrimination is justified may arise from a number of circumstances or considerations such as rumors, gossip, complaints of damage or through general inquiries

[68] Can. 2214, § 2.

[69] Can. 1552, § 2, n. 2.

[70] Can. 1552, § 2, n. 1.

[71] Can. 1933, § 1.

[72] Canons 1939-1946; Cf. Lega-Bartoccetti, *Commentarius,* Vol. III, Tit. XIX, cap. II, pp. 222-245; Coronata, *Manuale Practicum Iuris Disciplinaris et Criminalis Regularium* (Rome: Marietti, 1938), pp. 82-86 (hereafter cited as *Manuale*); Chelodi, *Ius Poenale* (Tridenti: Libr. Edit. Tridentum, 1925 [1920?]), pp. 157-159, n. 118.

of the ordinary.[73] The inquisitor or investigator collects material relative to the case, and when he has gathered a sufficient amount, or when it is impossible to find more, he adds an unbiased judgment on his findings and turns the entire case over to the ordinary.

It devolves upon the ordinary to determine whether the case should proceed to a criminal trial, or whether a judicial rebuke or precept will suffice to reclaim the culprit from his delinquency. But the norms for this determination are clearly set forth in three hypotheses in canon 1946, § 2. First, if the denunciation or incrimination appears to lack a solid foundation, a declaration to that effect must be issued and appended to the acts of the investigation, and all these documents must be placed in the secret archives. If, on the other hand, indications actually point to a crime, but at the same time do not suffice to warrant a criminal trial, these acts likewise should be placed in the secret archives.

The conduct of the accused should be watched, and if the ordinary deems it advisable he may give the accused a hearing in the matter and, if the case warrants, he may give a canonical admonition according to canon 2307. Finally, if the arguments seem certain or at least probably sufficient for the instituting of a criminal trial, he may cite the culprit to appear in court, and then proceed with the trial, or he may, if the case warrants, suspend the cleric in view of a duly certified possession of knowledge regarding the matter (*ex informata conscientia*).

In the first two hypotheses the demand of the law that the acts be preserved in the secret archives illustrates the care and solicitude of the Church to guard the rights of every individual, and yet to maintain an efficient administration of justice. If the supposed culprit has not been proved guilty, he has a strict right to his good name. Therefore, the provisions requiring these unproved allegations to be placed in the secret archives serves the purpose of keeping the inquisitorial proceedings outside the arena of public use. Coronata sees an additional advantage in the fact that, if any new elements occur, the inquisitorial proceedings can be examined again for further judgment, so that thereby there is obviated the need of another investigation.[74]

---

[73] Can. 1939, § 1.

[74] Coronata, *Manuale,* p. 85, n. 182.

If a case should eventuate in a formal trial, the law still provides for the careful custody of important documents. Canon 1645 permits the judge in criminal cases to decree that a document be retained by the tribunal if this is demanded by the common good. Furthermore, such documents are to be placed in the archives of the curia, that is, in the public or the secret archives as the nature of the case suggests. Ouce again, the law seeks to relegate confidential material to a special depository as a safeguard.

Canonists discuss the problem concerning the private, secret deliberations of the tribunal prior to the pronouncement of a sentence. The question hinges on the *secretum servandum* as adverted to in canon 1623, § 2, and 1871 § 2. Connolly, in commenting on the strict admonition of secrecy in these two canons, believes that its purpose probably is that of permitting the judges of the tribunal to engage in a free and unlimited discussion of the merits of the cause without the fear of criticism or embarrassment that might result if the deliberations were made public. The very thought of a possible publicity might influence the judges in their respective decisions.[75] He rightly points out that these secret deliberations and conclusions are not *acta causae* in the same sense as the rest of the judicial proofs, testimony, decrees, etc., and therefore these deliberations should be enclosed in a separate folio and preserved apart from the other judicial acts.[76]

Beyond the prescription of canon 1871, § 2, one may point to Article 203, § 1, of the Matrimonial Instruction of 1936, which requires the *vota iudicum* to be kept in the secret archives.[77] It is probable that the special secret archives here mentioned are to be understood as archives distinct from the diocesan secret archives. Doheny accepts the words of the Instruction as referring to the special archives of the tribunal.[78] In fact, Vaughan urges the tribunal to have

---

[75] *Appeals,* The Catholic University of America Canon Law Studies, n. 79 (Washington, D. C.; The Catholic University of America, 1932), p. 97.

[76] *Ibidem,* p. 98.

[77] S. C. Sacr., *Instructio Servanda a Tribunalibus Dioecesanis in Pertractandis Causis de Nullitate Matrimoniorum,* 15 aug., 1936: "*Vota iudicum actis causae adiungi non debent, neque ad tribunal appellationis sunt transmittenda, sed in speciali archivo secreto servanda, saltem per decennium. Quo elapso fas erit ea comburere.*"—*AAS,* XXVIII (1936), 352.

[78] *Canonical Procedure in Matrimonial Cases,* Vol. I, *Formal Judicial Procedure* (2. ed., Milwaukee: Bruce Publishing Co., 1948), p. 486.

its own special secret archives for these *vota iudicum* as well as for documents of pending secret causes.[79]

Vaughan likewise urges that when secret causes are completed they should be sealed in an envelope and filed in the diocesan archives. This seems to be in complete harmony with the purpose of the secret archives of the diocese as indicated in the Code law.[80] Therefore, if this judicial material, namely the *vota iudicum* and the documents of pending secret causes, is not too bulky and can be preserved in the special secret archives of the tribunal, the ordinary may permit the maintenance of such archives. For completed cases, however, the *vota iudicum* and the entire *acta* should be transferred to the secret archives of the diocese in accordance with canon 379, § 1.

Section 2. Extrajudicial Procedures

There are instances when a formal trial is not necessary,[81] or is impossible,[82] or is forbidden.[83] In such cases the Church permits an extrajudicial method in the exercise of its coercive power. Thus, if the crime was certain and notorious, there is no need for a formal process, since the object of such a process has already been attained. That object was the gathering of evidence which is sufficient either for the condemnation of the culprit or his exoneration. The ordinary may therefore immediately inflict the penal sanction expressed in the law or the precept. But even if no definite sanction has been enacted, the existence of a special gravity in the transgression as well as the emergence of notable scandal upon its commission would warrant the ordinary's use of canon 2222, § 1.[84]

---

[79] *Constitutions for Diocesan Courts,* The Catholic University of America Canon Law Studies, n. 210 (Washington, D. C.: The Catholic University of America Press, 1944), p. 49, nn. 95-96.

[80] *Ibidem,* p. 48, n. 94.

[81] E. g., if the crime was notorious, or if there was conclusive evidence to incriminate the culprit for his misdeed.

[82] E. g., if the civil authorities interfere.

[83] E. g., if the crime or delict was occult. Canon 1933, § 1, specifies that only public crimes may be prosecuted before an ecclesiastical tribunal.

[84] Casey, *A Study of Canon 2222,* § 1, The Catholic University of America Canon Law Studies, n. 290 (Washington, D. C.: The Catholic University of America Press, 1949), pp. 86-89.

The documents of these extrajudicial procedures should be preserved in the same way as was determined for formal trials. Since there is no express statute on the matter, by virtue of canon 20 the ordinary can follow the norm of canon 1645, § 2. Therefore, whatever document should be preserved ought to be placed in either the public or the secret archives, depending on the nature of the case.[85]

When there is question of an occult crime or even a public crime in difficult exceptional cases, the Code has instituted another extrajudicial procedure which applies solely to the extraordinary means of punishment, called the suspension *ex informata conscientia*.[86] This procedure follows upon the inquisitional procedure already discussed. If the suspension is invoked, then by virtue of canon 2142 a signed record of the acts must be kept in the archives.

Murphy maintains that two copies of the decree of suspension should be made, one copy to be preserved in the secret archives, and the other copy to be given to the cleric who is suspended.[87] He further notes: "In all cases where possible it would be well to have the copy of the decree which is deposited in the Secret Archives signed by the suspended cleric.[88]

Section 3. Penal Remedies

In dealing with less serious delinquencies, the Church has enacted certain disciplinary measures known in law as penal remedies and intended as preventive procedures to avert the lapse into grave offenses. The penal character of these remedies presupposes some offense or something proximate to an offense, and the reality of this offense must always be verified extrajudicially. This investigation may be secret or public, formal or informal, according to the case.[89]

Canon 2309, § 5, demands that both penal remedies, admonitions or warnings as well as rebukes or reprimands (*monitio et correptio*), even though

---

[85] Coronata, *Manuale*, p. 19, n. 30.

[86] Canons 2186-2194.

[87] *Suspension ex Informata Conscientia*, the Catholic University of America Canon Law Studies, n. 76 (Washington, D. C.: The Catholic University of America, 1932), p. 103 (hereafter cited as Murphy); Abbo-Hannan, II, 777-778.

[88] *Ibidem*, p. 104.

[89] Cf. Ayrinhac-Lydon, *Penal Legislation* (Rev. ed., New York: Benziger Brothers, 1936), pp. 134-139.

they be administered secretly, must be susceptible to proof through a document to be preserved in the secret archives of the curia. Dougherty points out that these documents can be brought out for any subsequent *inquisitio* if the same delinquent is denounced for another offense.[90]

No special formalities are prescribed for that penal remedy that is known as the canonical precept or injunction (*praeceptum*). Ayrinhac-Lydon believe this to be so inasmuch as the formalities are substantially the same with the ones prescribed for the canonical reprimand which precedes it.[91] Esswein is more exact canonically by citing canons 24 and 2225 together with Article VIII of the Instruction of 1880 as the norms of procedure in the issuing of a canonical precept.[92] He further adds: "The record of the transaction should be signed by the parties present, also by the delinquent himself, although he is not obliged to do so. The record is then filed in the archives."[93]

The requirement of canon 2309, § 5, namely that the records of the warning and the reprimand as penal remedies be placed in the secret archives, furnishes reason for concluding that the same procedure should be followed in the case of the canonical precept. Therefore the archives cited by the authors undoubtedly point to secret archives.

The final penal remedy, vigilance or surveillance (*vigilantia*), follows upon the imposition of a canonical precept. The vigilance considered here is not the ordinary vigilance incumbent upon the ordinary in watching over every member of his flock. Here the question is one of a specially and a particularly close surveillance, which serves actually as an exceptional remedy for determining whether the ordinary's canonical precept has been violated, and, if so, when, where, and before whom. This vigilance likewise follows the norms of canon 2309, and records of it must be preserved in the secret archives.

The norms of canon 2309 apply to all four penal remedies, and not merely to the canonical warning and the canonical reprimand, as a cursory glance at

---

[90] *De Inquisitione Speciali,* The Catholic University of America Canon Law Studies, n. 213 (Washington, D. C.: The Catholic University of America Press, 1945), p. 167.

[91] *Penal Legislation,* p. 138.

[92] *Extrajudicial Coercive Powers of Ecclesiastical Superiors,* The Catholic University of America Canon Law Studies, n. 127 (Washington, D. C.: The Catholic University of America Press, 1941), p. 106.

[93] *Loc. cit.*

the canon might seem to indicate. The footnotes in the Code indicate that one of the principal sources for this canon was the Instruction of 1880 as issued by the Sacred Congregation of Bishops and Regulars. In treating of the formalities to be observed in the use of the principal penal remedies of the time, the Instruction demanded that there be some documentary proof of the execution (of the remedies).[94]

As Lega (1860-1935) pointed out, it was essential that the execution (of the penal remedies) be such that it could be proved *in foro externo,* if that became necessary in the future.[95] And in speaking of the canonical precept, he maintained that all proofs of the case should be preserved in the archives in response to the possible need of them in the event that an appeal was interposed.[96]

There seems to be little doubt, therefore, that the law as it exists in the Code today is substantially the same as the pre-Code legislation. Furthermore, the nature of the penal remedies in question postulates the same understanding of the law.

Therefore in the light of the express requirements of the law in criminal matters as well as in view of the traditional *modus agendi* of the Church in penal and judicial questions, it is evident that every attempt should be made with a view also to the correction rather than simply the punishment of the delinquents. Now, all the procedures involved in these remedial measures as well as in the enforcement of severe penalties were to be made available in documentary form in the event of further examination or investigation. Whenever, then, the nature of the case demanded more than ordinary secrecy, the secret archives were to serve as the ecclesiastical safeguard.

This study has considered only those statutes which expressly demand the use of the secret archives for criminal matters, and does not attempt to discuss all the various crimes which would imply a similar procedure for their records and documents. An exhaustive presentation of the specific crimes which in

[94] S. C. Ep. et Reg., instr. *Sacra haec,* 11 iun. 1880, n. 6: ". . . *ita tamen ut de earundem executione constet ex aliquo actu.*"—*Fontes,* n. 2005.

[95] *De Iudiciis Ecclesiasticis* (4 vols., Romae: Typis Vaticanis, 1896-1901), IV, n. 183, p. 247.

[96] ". . . *et ab Ordinario probationes inde collectae religiossime asservandae sunt in archivio pro necessitate forsan exoritura satisfaciendi iudicio appellationis.*"—*Loc. cit.*

consequence of the penal section of the Code postulate the use of the secret archives would be cumbersome to this study, and furthermore would not add to an understanding of the nature and function of the secret archives. But by an analysis of the express legislation on secret archives, it is felt that the mind of the Church will be more readily understood, and could be adapted to particular circumstances in those questions for which there is no precise determination in ecclesiastical law.[97]

Article IV. Additional Secret Material

With reference to the contents of the secret archives, attention has been given to the materials determined by law and also to a few implied in the law. In the administration of his diocese the ordinary may find other materials which ought to be preserved in the secret archives because of some special circumstance. These will generally center around occult matters, matters of infamy or matters of exceptional secrecy. Besides the materials described in this article, the minutes of the meetings of the diocesan consultors could, for example, be singled out.[98]

While generally there is a certain amount of secrecy attached to the matters discussed in the meeting of the diocesan consultors, such material can be preserved in the general or common archives of the diocese. If, on the other hand, some particularly confidential matter was discussed, the ordinary may prefer to preserve it in the secret archives. How long is such material to remain in the secret archives? That will depend on the nature of the matter as well as the need. The ordinary is the judge of this, and he it is who determines the entire procedure. But if he does commit the minutes of the meeting or a part of those minutes to the secret archives, he ought to observe the pertinent norms regarding the inventory.

---

[97] For examples of careful studies wherein general principles have been analyzed, including the principles regarding documents and records, in relation to these criminal procedures, cf. Rainer, *Suspension of Clerics,* The Catholic University of America Canon Law Studies, n. 111 (Washington, D. C.: The Catholic University of America, 1937); Meier, *Penal Administrative Procedure against Negligent Pastors,* The Catholic University of America Canon Law Studies, n. 140 (Washington, D. C.: The Catholic University of America Press, 1941).

[98] Louis, p. 72.

Matters pertaining to the Holy Office as well as any highly confidential correspondence with any of the Sacred Congregations may likewise be preserved in the secret archives.

In all these cases the ordinary is free to determine his mode of action. He should be guided by the norms discussed above for such cases as are determined in the law.

Section 1. Baptismal Records of Adopted Persons

It has been suggested that perhaps the diocesan secret archives should be utilized for the complete baptismal record of adopted children.[99] In order to have an accurate, reliable and complete record which nevertheless will not be so available that it could thereby bring anguish or ill-fame to anyone, the local ordinary could use the secret archives for these records. While Monsignor Arthur finds such a method less convenient, nevertheless, if the correct information must be kept without detriment to the parties, the writer believes the *mens legislatoris* would extend the use of the secret archives to include baptismal information which is at least relatively secret.

Since chanceries require a duplicate record of all baptisms and marriages in the diocese, it is not uncommon that copies of these records are obtained directly from the chancery. And therefore, if the records of adopted persons are obtained from the chancery, it would not generally cause a loss of repute to the adopted person. The parish of the baptism could be permitted to retain simply the essential information noted in canon 777, § 1, giving the adopted name of the baptized and the names of the adoptive parents. A notation in the record should indicate the need of consulting the chancery for additional information, namely for purposes of matrimony, Holy Orders, and religious profession.

The chancery record should contain the complete record of the adopted person, inasmuch as some of this information, because of civil laws or because of special circumstances, may never be available in public documentary form. Nevertheless the essential information will be available to the local ordinary when he needs, e. g., to determine the status of legitimacy for ordination, or for entrance into a religious community, or to ascertain the extant relationship through consanguinity or affinity at the time the parties contemplate the contracting of a marriage.

---

[99] Arthur, "Baptismal Certificates for Adopted Children," *The Jurist*, XIII (1953), 76.

The question of the inconvenience of the secret archives is, of course, not unlikely. Although in law the local ordinary is given complete custody of the diocesan secret archives,[100] it is possible for the chancellor or some other delegated priest to assist with the work connected with the secret archives.[101] Since these baptismal records of adopted persons should be kept in a special register separate from other secret archives material, and since the chancellor is by his very office the principal archivist-notary of the diocese,[102], and since his office obliges him to observe secrecy,[103] he is the logical delegate to enter these records in the register and to issue certificates of them according to the need.

Canon 384, § 2, demands that chancellors, pastors and other custodians of archives, in giving access to documents and in making and delivering copies of them, shall observe the rules enacted by lawful ecclesiastical authority and, in a case of doubt, shall consult the local ordinary. In view of this canon, the writer believes that the ordinary should enact rules to govern the proper keeping of baptismal records of adopted persons in his territory. These rules should seek to protect the interest of the Church as well as the interests of the adopted. The use of the secret archives as the depository for these records can frequently serve the situation best, especially in those states where civil legislation or the practice of the civil courts is apt to conflict with the laws or requirements of the Church.

Section 2. Beatification and Canonization Acts

The ordinary processes of the Code governing the construction of beatification and canonization causes are of such a nature that at times they seem to imply the use of the secret archives of the diocese. Thus, canon 2041, § 2, demands that in these ordinary processes after every session the acts must be closed and sealed with the seal of the judge or the tribunal of the diocese, and may not be opened again until the judge has, in the next session, examined the seal and found it entire and intact.

If it is evident that the seal has been tampered with, the judge shall refer the matter to the Sacred Congregation (of Rites). Between the sessions, says

[100] Can. 379, § 4; Louis, p. 82.
[101] Coronate, Vol. I-II, p. 499, footnote n. 1.
[102] Can. 372, § 1.
[103] Can. 364, § 2, n. 3; Prince, p. 58.

Blaher, the acts are in the care of the notary, who must keep them in some safe place, usually in the diocesan archives.[104] It is true that the ordinary diocesan archives generally would be adequate, but if the local ordinary feels that the interim between sessions are of such a duration, or the material and the testimony in the acts are of such importance, that they would demand any additional safeguards, he can require that these acts be placed in the secret archives.

When the entire process is completed, a transcript or copy of the acts must be made. This transcript must, according to canon 2054, be written out in longhand. The reason given is the desire of the Holy See that only two sets of the acts exist, the original in the archives of the diocesan curia, and the copy in the archives of the Sacred Congregation of Rites.[105] This regulation seems to strengthen the contention that special and extraordinary concern is demanded for these acts of the process. While a decree in 1889 of the Sacred Congregation of Rites required simply that the original acts be kept "*in archivo episcopali,*"[106] the essential secrecy as well as the *mens legislatoris* seem to postulate more than ordinary care. This is likewise implied in the words of canon 2056, § 1.[107]

It is true that no obligation is placed by the Code on the local ordinary to keep these acts in the secret archives of the diocese, but it seems more prudent and more in harmony with the nature of these processes to give the acts the best protection afforded by canon law. This will be particularly true when the case is concluded and the transcript of the acts has been forwarded to the Holy See. The original acts are of great importance, especially as long as the only other copy is still in transit. Therefore the very nature of the acts demands more than ordinary care and custody.

Section 3. Documents to be Burned

Can. 379, § 1—. . . *In eo* (*archivo secreto*) *scripturae secreto servandae cautissime custodiantur; sed singulis annis quamprimum comburantur docu-*

---

[104] *The Ordinary Processes in Causes of Beatification and Canonization,* The Catholic University of America Canon Law Studies, n. 268 (Washington, D. C.: The Catholic University of America Press, 1949), p. 196.

[105] *Ibidem,* p. 215.

[106] S. R. C., decr., 8 apr. 1889—*Fontes,* n. 6194.

[107] "*Absoluta collatione, archetypum clauditur et sigillis munitur in archivo Curiae diligenter asservandum et numquam aperiendum sine venia Sedis Apostolicae.*"

menta causarum criminalium in materia morum, quarum rei vita cesserint vel quae a decennio sententia condemnatoria absolutae sunt, retento facti brevi summario cum textu sententiae definitivae.

While the Church will not be remiss in invoking the sanctions of the law upon delinquents, nevertheless the legislator makes provision that the details of even the worst crimes may not be perpetually preserved against the regained good reputation of a delinquent. Therefore the law demands that annually some secret archives documents of criminal cases regarding bad behavior be burned. This is to be done after the death of the delinquent, or also when ten years have elapsed after the condemnatory sentence had been imposed.

The *quamprimum* of canon 379, § 1, has been variously interpreted. According to Louis the documents should be burned "as soon as possible after the death of the guilty party or after the lapse of ten years from the pronouncement of his condemnatory sentence."[108] Archbishop Mathias seems to offer a better understanding of the canon when he translates the passage of "Each year, as early as possible . . ."[109] The intent, therefore, of the canon is rather to urge that the annual obligation be fulfilled *quamprimum.* Not only the seriousness of the law but also the proper significance of the word *quamprium* in its text and context[110] is better understood if one follows Mathias' interpretation.

Authors also point out that, since the law prescribes the burning of the documents, the mere tearing of them to shreds, or the destroying of them in any other way, would not fulfill the law.[111] The reason for the destruction is the evident desire to protect the reputation of the delinquents,[112] especially if they are deceased.[113] An additional motive is the avoidance of all useless and dangerous multiplication of papers.[114] Louis adds a very cogent reason, namely "that timely destruction of the documents may prevent scandal and avoid unjust, unnecessary and embarrassing attacks upon the Church, by making it impossible for such documents to fall into the hands of her enemies."[115]

---

[108] Louis, p. 72.
[109] Mathias, p. 280.
[110] Can. 18.
[111] D'Angelo, p. 111; Mathias, p. 280; Louis, p. 73.
[112] Louis, p. 72.
[113] Mathias, p. 280.
[114] D'Angelo, p. 111.
[115] Louis, p. 72.

Would it ever be permitted to burn these documents sooner or earlier than the law requires or contemplates? In the event of an imminent danger to the Church or to the individual, the ordinary would be justified in anticipating the fulfillment of the law. And, if the case warrants it, even the brief summary along with the text of the definitive sentence could be destroyed, or for an equal reason the making of this summary could be omitted.

The phrase *"causarum criminalium"* of the canon includes reference not only to the acts of criminal trials, but also to the acts of extrajudicial cases and to the documents pertaining to penal remedies.

Ayrinhac (1867-1930) thought that the rule of burning the documents did not apply if no condemnation had been pronounced.[116] This does not, however, seem to be in harmony with the intent of the rule. The rule calls for the burning of these documents in two situations, either when the culprit has died (and nothing is said here about a condemnatory sentence) or when ten years have elapsed after the condemnatory sentence had been imposed. In the latter instance, it is true, the canon specifically names the condemnatory sentence. But this specification merely singles out the climax of the *causa* as the starting point for the computation of the postulated lapse of time.

If the decision of the ordinary or of the judge in the case is actually not a condemnatory sentence, e. g., merely a canonical admonition or warning, nevertheless the rule for the burning of the documents would apply, and the computation analagously would commence with that decision of the ordinary or of the judge. This explanation, in fine, seems to approach the purpose of the canon more perfectly. Furthermore, the ten years after the condemnatory sentence are to be computed according to the canonical norms of canon 34, § 3, nn. 1 and 3.

Although the law requires the burning of these documents, a brief summary of the case along with the text of the final sentence must be preserved.[117] Perhaps this is to be done in protection of the Church against future legal action on the part of the delinquent or his relatives.[118] In any case, the ordinary is gravely held to comply with these obligations relating to the documents of criminal cases. Not only as custodian of the archives but likewise as adminis-

[116] *Constitution of the Church* (New York: Longmans, Green and Co., 1929), p. 219.

[117] Mathias, p. 281.

[118] Louis, p. 73.

trator of the diocese committed to him, the ordinary is obliged to protect the interests of the Church as well as of the individuals who are in some way or other subject to his government.

In 1941 the Code Commission was asked if the words of canon 379, § 1: "*retento facti brevi summario cum textu sententiae definitivae*" are to be applied only to cases which have been closed by a condemnatory sentence for ten years, or also to cases in which the accused have departed this life. The Commission replied in the affirmative to the first part, and in the negative to the second.[119]

This reply leaves no doubt therefore that, when the delinquent dies, all the documents of his case are to be destroyed and not even a summary of the case along with the text of the final sentence is to be retained. The reply likewise implies that, when the summary along with the text of the sentence has been kept after the lapse of the ten-year period during which the fuller documents themselves had been preserved, it is in turn to be burned when the delinquent dies.

Section 4. Inventory

Can. 379, § 2: "*Etiam huius secreti archivi vel armarii inventarium seu catalogus conficiatur ad normam can. 375, § 2.*"

An inventory of the documents in the secret archives must be kept, but an inventory in the sense of canon 379, § 2, is more than a mere index or list of the documents. This is evident from the reference back to canon 375, § 2, which treats of the inventory for the general or common archives. The important phrase in that earlier canon is "*cum brevi singularum scripturarum synopsi.*" This summary of the case or of the document is essential to the inventory.

It was already seen in the historical section what degree of importance many of the Councils attached to these *inventaria.* Detailed regulations, for example, were invoked for the safeguarding of these *inventaria,* not only because they were lists of the documents in the archives, but especially because they included a careful description of the contents of the documents.[120] A comparison therefore of the pre-Code practice with the norm of canon 375, § 2, which

[119] Pont. Comm. Intr., 5 aug. 1941—*AAS,* XXXIII (1941), 378; Cf. Bouscaren, *Digest,* II, 132.

[120] *Supra,* p. 39.

requires a synopsis of the documents leads to the conclusion that a mere index of the documents does not fulfill the law.

This may seem like a superfluous prescription, and yet on further scrutiny one sees indicated the primary purpose of the secret archives. The contents of the secret archives are entrusted to the ordinary for the better administration of his diocese. These confidential documents are confided to his care to be used only when it becomes absolutely necessary. It should never be demanded of him that all these documents be examined even at great intervals. An examination of the inventory as it is here described reveals the nature of the documents in the secret archives, and thereby the ordinary will understand in a general way what confidential material has been entrusted to him. And even more important is the consideration that the ordinary will then recognize what documents should be removed and burned.

An inventory is required for the general or common archives of the diocese.[121] The inventory for the secret archives will follow the same norms. This inventory is preserved in the secret archives to serve for the facility and the convenience of the ordinary. Therefore there is no need for any additional precautions regarding the information given in the synopsis of the inventory. The synopsis must be precisely that, a succinct statement.

This inventory must be kept up-to-date. Since it will be only on rare occasions that additional documents are placed in the secret archives, the ordinary would probably find it simpler and easier to attend to the inventory immediately. Otherwise an annual or biennial check would suffice.

Regarding the matters entered in special registers, it will not be necessary to keep an additional inventory. The alphabetical index in the register plus the nature of the material recorded in that register will serve the purpose of an inventory.[122] But for other material the inventory will serve not only as an index but also as a conspectus of the cases involved. And this inventory should indicate how to locate the docket or document in the midst of others. That is why a system in filing is needed. What system should be used will depend on the quantity of the documents in the archives as well as on the variety of the cases. The ordinary must use his own discretion in his method of filing, and it is to his advantage that it be a workable and adaptable system.

---

[121] Can. 375, § 2.

[122] E. g., the register for marriages of conscience, dispensations from occult irregularities and impediments.

CHAPTER V. CUSTODY OF THE SECRET ARCHIVES

Article I. Custody of the Keys

Can. 379, § 3: "*Hoc archivum vel armarium duabus clavibus inter se diversis aperiatur, . . .*"

Since the common law seeks to be as inclusive and comprehensive as possible, and since the importance of the secret archives demands especial care for the archives, the Code gives detailed regulations in order to safeguard the contents of the secret archives. The need for two different keys is the essential means chosen to guarantee authorized entrance alone to the secret archives. The custody of each of these keys is specifically determined no matter who may legitimately be responsible for the administration of the diocese.

The entrance to the secret archives, therefore, must be provided with a lock requiring two different keys to open it.[1] Some writers believe that two distinct locks are demanded by the law,[2] but this is not necessarily so. Many modern safes and vaults are equipped with a single lock that requires the use of a combination and a key. As will be seen later, such a safe would be highly practical for the purposes it serves. That the keys, or combinations, must be unlike is evident from the wording of canon 379, § 3.

If a combination or two different combinations are used, then these should be changed periodically. This could easily be done at the time of the servicing of the locks as described in Chapter III, Article II.

Section 1. When the See is Occupied

Can. 379, § 3: "Hoc archivium vel armarium duabus clavibus inter se diversis aperiatur, quarum altera apud Episcopum vel Administratorem Apostolicum, altera apud Vicarium Generalem vel, eo deficiente, Curiae cancellarium asservetur."

The clear determination in the law regarding the custodian of each of the two keys leaves no doubt about the strict intent of the law. The local ordinary,

[1] Ayrinhac, *Constitution of the Church,* p. 220.

[2] E. g., Abbo-Hannan, I, 394; Louis, p. 76.

as the immediate shepherd and administrator of the diocese, has not only the right but also the duty to govern his diocese in spiritual and temporal matters.[3] And therefore the diocesan secret archives are expressly committed to his care, and he should not delegate this control unless grave reasons warrant it. He must retain the principal key.

While the canon simply employs the term "bishop," it is evident that the episcopal local ordinary is meant. Coadjutor or auxiliary bishops are not included. The bishop who governs the diocese is the bishop envisioned in this statute.

The Sovereign Pontiff, for weighty and special reasons, sometimes entrusts either for a limited time or permanently the government of a canonically erected diocese, either during the incumbency of the ordinary or during a vacancy of the see, to an apostolic administrator.[4] If such an apostolic administrator is permanently appointed to administer a diocese, he has all the rights and duties of a residential bishop.[5] If his appointment is for a limited time, then he receives all the rights and duties of a vicar capitular.[6]

One may ask whether the term "apostolic administrator" of canon 379, § 3, applies only to the one permanently appointed, or likewise to one appointed for a limited term. Both Louis and McDonough maintain that the temporary apostolic administrator is included in the scope of the canon, but they furnish different arguments for their doctrine.

Louis cites the canonical distinctions given in canon 315, §§ 1 and 2, pertaining to the permanent and the temporary apostolic administrators, as the basis for his reasoning.[7] As already seen, the one enjoys the same rights as a residential bishop while the other has the rights of a vicar capitular. In the canons dealing with secret archives, no distinction of permanent or temporary administrator is made. Louis argues that if the rights which the canons confer in reference to secret archives were meant only for the permanent apostolic administrator, every mention of that official would be superfluous, since the permanent apostolic administrator would already have these rights,

---

[3] Can. 335, § 1.

[4] Can. 312; Abbo-Hannan, I, 342.

[5] Can. 315, § 1.

[6] Can. 315, § 2, n. 1.

[7] *Diocesan Archives*, p. 74.

along with all the other rights of a residential bishop. Therefore, since the law here mentions the apostolic administrator without distinction, the law seems to give every apostolic administrator, permanent or temporary, the same rights as a residential bishop in this matter.

McDonough's argument is based on canon 382, §§ 1 and 2, which restricts the power of the vicar capitular with reference to the secret archives, but does not mention the temporary apostolic administrator.[8] While his argumentation is not clearly worked out, it substantially corroborates the stand of Monsignor Louis. If the temporary apostolic administrator enjoyed the same rights as the vicar capitular with reference to the secret archives, then the canon would logically mention him together with the vicar capitular, just as the previous canon mentioned the apostolic administrator together with the residential bishop.

The two arguments, therefore, are based on the mention of the apostolic administrator without reference to his permanent or temporary appointment and on the lack of a clear distinction between this apostolic administrator and either the residential bishop or the vicar capitular. Both arguments sufficiently prove that not only the permanent but also the temporary apostolic administrator is given the same rights over the secret archives as a residential bishop.

The residential bishop or the apostolic administrator must retain the principal key to the secret archives. The other key is to be kept by the vicar-general, or by the chancellor "when the diocese has no vicar general."[9]

Should a diocese have more than one vicar-general, the bishop may designate the one who is to have charge of the key to the secret archives.[10] Canon 366, § 3, permits more than one vicar-general only if the diversity of rites or the extensiveness of the diocese demands it. If two or more vicar-generals are appointed because of the diversity of rites, the bishop would more likely commit the second key of the secret archives to that vicar-general whose rite predominates in the diocese. If the extensiveness of the diocese warrants the appointment of an additional vicar-general at a distance from the see city, the bishop

---

[8] *Apostolic Administrators,* The Catholic University of America Canon Law Studies, n. 139 (Washington, D. C.: The Catholic University of America Press, 1941), pp. 108-110.

[9] Ayrinhac, *Constitution of the Church,* p. 220.

[10] Louis, p. 76.

would more conveniently commit the second key to the vicar-general who resides nearest the office or who frequents it most.

Although the Code does not permit a vicar apostolic or a prefect apostolic to appoint a vicar-general, Benedict XV (1914-1922) granted them the power to appoint a vicar delegate, who would have the same jurisdiction that vicar-generals of residential bishops have under the Code.[11] Therefore these vicars delegate enjoys the same rights as the vicar-generals also in reference to the secret archives. Coronata hesitantly admits this,[12] but the concession of Benedict XV leaves no doubt whatsoever. Louis is surely mistaken when he says the key could be held by the pro-vicar or the pro-prefect.[13]

The chancellor would hold the key only if there is no vicar-general. But the phrase *eo deficiente* in the canon points not merely to a vacancy in the office of vicar-general, but likewise to the absence of the vicar-general for any length of time.[14] The vicar-general is chosen to hold the second key because the law presumes that he is available to the bishop in the administration of the diocese.[15] If for some reason or another he is not available, then the law provides for someone else who is likewise presumed to be available because of his office. But this latter person, the chancellor, would function in this capacity only if and when the vicar-general is not available (*eo deficiente*).[16]

An additional provision to safeguard the secret archives imposes an obligation on the bishop to appoint a priest to assume custody of his key whenever the see becomes vacant or impeded.

Can. 380—Statim a capta possessione, Episcopus sacerdotem designet, qui, sede vacante aut impedita, clavem secreti tabularii seu armarii quae apud Episcopum erat, assumat.

A bishop takes canonical possession of his diocese according to the norms of canon 334, § 3. Among his duties at that time is the appointment of a special

---

[11] S. C. Prop. Fide, ep. 8 dec. 1919—*AAS,* XII (1920), 120; Cf. Bouscaren, *Digest,* I, 144.

[12] *Institutiones,* I, p. 499, footnote n. 5.

[13] *Diocesan Archives,* p. 76.

[14] Blat. *Commentarium Textus Codicis Iuris Canonici* (6 vols., Vol. II [Lib. II, pars I], 2. ed., Romae, 1921), II, p. 409, n. 415.

[15] Can. 369, § 1.

[16] Prince, pp. 76-77.

priest according to canon 380. The *statim* of the canon evidently suggests that he do not postpone this appointment indefinitely. Again one sees the solicitude of the Church to protect these secret archives from any misuse by unauthorized persons.

The appointment should be in writing and in two copies, one to remain in the general archives and the other to be given to the priest himself. When the see is impeded or vacant the priest is able to assert his right to the episcopal key to the secret archives. And, further, when he presents the key to the bishop's successor he can prove his right to have had possession of it up to then. And finally, in appointing this priest the bishop should indicate where and how the priest can obtain the key when the occasion arises.[17]

Section 2. When the See is Impeded

Can. 381, § 1—Nisi Administrator Apostolicus dioecesi datus fuerit:

1° Sede impedita ad normam can. 429, § 1, sacerdos ab Episcopo designatus, si quidem regimen dioecesis sit penes virum ecclesiasticum ab Episcopo delegatum, clavem eidem remittat; si penes Vicarium Generalem, eam ipse retineat;

2° Sede vero vacante aut impedita ad normam cit. can. 429, § 3, idem sacerdos clavem remittat Vicario Capitulari statim post eius designationem; Vicarius vero Generalis vel cancellarius aliam clavem a se retentam remittere eodem tempore debet primae Capituli dignitati vel consultori dioecesano munere antiquiori.

A residential bishop may at times be impeded from the actual government of his diocese. In such a case the see is said to be quasi-vacant, since the bishop is prevented from exercising jurisdiction in person.[18] Canons 312 and 429, § 1, make provision for the diocese if the see is quasi-vacant as a result of the bishop's captivity, banishment, exile or disability, and if he is so impeded that he cannot communicate with his diocese even by letters.[19] And the canons pertaining to the secret archives likewise provide for every possible security for the secret archives if the see becomes quasi-vacant.

---

[17] Louis, p. 78; Mathias, pp. 281-282.

[18] Abbo-Hannan, I, 429.

[19] Cf. McDonough, pp. 69-72.

A quasi-vacant diocese may be governed by the vicar-general or by a priest who has been delegated by the bishop for this purpose, or by an apostolic administrator.

When a diocese becomes quasi-vacant or impeded, then the priest appointed by the bishop to assume the custody of the episcopal key to the secret archives, according to canon 380, must immediately fulfill his obligation. He should assume the episcopal key according to his appointment, and as soon as the bishop's successor takes over the administration of the diocese present the key to the person designated by law.

The law envisions several situations in which the administration of the diocese would devolve upon any of several persons if the diocese is impeded:

a) If an apostolic administrator is sent to the diocese, he receives the same right that the residential bishop possesses with respect to the secret archives. Therefore, if the priest contemplated in canon 380 has assumed the bishop's key to the secret archives, he must turn it over to the apostolic administrator as soon as the latter begins to govern the diocese. If he actually has not yet assumed the key personally, he is still obliged to see that the apostolic administrator learns where and how to obtain the key.

b) If the administration of the diocese devolves upon the vicar-general, then the law provides that the priest of canon 380 keep the episcopal key to the secret archives himself.

c) If, according to canon 366, § 3, the vicar-general is absent or impeded, and another ecclesiastic delegated by the bishop administers the diocese, this ecclesiastic would receive the bishop's key to the secret archives from the priest whom the law mentions in canon 380.

d) If the vicar-general is absent or impeded and no other ecclesiastic has been delegated by the bishop as administrator, the cathedral chapter (or diocesan consultors) must elect a vicar capitular. This vicar capitular (diocesan administrator) becomes the local ordinary, and to him must be given the bishop's key to the secret archives.

The disposition of the second key will likewise depend on who succeeds to the administration of the diocese when the see is impeded. Up to the time the see became impeded, the key was held by the vicar-general or chancellor, as already seen.

a) If an apostolic administrator is sent to the diocese, the jurisdiction of the residential bishop and his vicar-general is suspended.[20] Vermeerch,[21] Campagna,[22] McDonough[23] and others believe that a permanent apostolic administrator can appoint a vicar-general, since he receives all the rights and duties of a residential bishop, which naturally include the power to elect a vicar-general. They likewise maintain that, since a temporary apostolic administrator resembles a vicar capitular,[24] he is unqualified to elect a vicar-general. Therefore, the ecclesiastic who was vicar-general to the impeded residential bishop and who held the second key to the secret archives must submit his key to one or the other of two persons. If the apostolic administrator is permanently appointed to the diocese and has chosen his own vicar-general, this new vicar-general must now assume the second key. If the apostolic administrator is permanently appointed and does not wish to elect a vicar-general at present, the second key should be given to the chancellor and later turned over to the vicar-general when one is appointed. If the apostolic administrator is appointed only temporarily to the impeded see, then, inasmuch as his status is equivalent to that of a vicar capitular, he will not have a vicar-general, and thus, as for the vicar capitular (or the diocesan administrator), the second key of the secret archives will be held by the ranking dignitary of the chapter (or the oldest diocesan consultor).

b) If the administration of the diocese devolves upon the vicar-general, then, as has been seen, he continues to hold his own key and the priest spoken of in canon 380 assumes and holds the bishop's key.

c) If the vicar-general himself is absent or impeded, and another ecclesiastic, according to canon 366, § 3, has been delegated by the residential bishop to administer the diocese, this delegate's status would be equivalent to that of a vicar capitular. And therefore, while he receives the bishop's key to the secret archives, the second key must be surrendered to the ranking dignitary of the chapter (or the senior diocesan consultor).

---

[20] McDonough, pp. 167-170.

[21] *"De Constitutione Vicarii Generalis vel Delegati facta ab Administratore Apostolico," Periodica,* XIII (1924), 15-17.

[22] *Il Vicario Generale del Vescovo,* The Catholic University of America Canon Law Studies, n. 66 (Washington, D. C.: The Catholic University of America, 1921), p. 90, footnote 14.

[23] *Apostolic Administrators,* pp. 152-158.

[24] Can. 315, § 2, n. 1.

d) If there is no one to assume the administration of the impeded diocese according to canons 312 and 429, § 1, then the diocesan consultors (or cathedral chapter) must elect a diocesan administrator (or vicar capitular).[25] He receives the bishop's key and the oldest diocesan consultor (or ranking capitular dignitary) receives the second key.

Wernz-Vidal make a pertinent observation with regard to the oldest diocesan consultor or the ecclesiastic who holds the highest dignity in the cathedral chapter. If this person is elected as vicar capitular, the second key to the secret archives should be given to the second dignitary in rank or the second oldest consultor. This provision is in complete harmony with the law which intends that the two keys be held by different persons.[26]

Section 3. When the See is Vacant

An episcopal see becomes vacant upon the death of the bishop, upon the latter's resignation accepted by the Roman Pontiff, upon the bishop's transfer to another see, and upon removal, provided of course that the bishop has received notice of it.[27] In the event of a bishop's transfer to another see, his first diocese (*sedes a qua*) becomes vacant, but by virtue of canon 430, § 3, n. 1, he continues to administer it until he takes canonical possession of his new diocese (*sedes ad quam*).

Unless an apostolic administrator has been appointed, or the Holy See has made some special provision, the government of a vacant diocese devolves upon the cathedral chapter (or board of diocesan consultors) which elects a vicar capitular (or diocesan administrator).[28] As soon as this vicar capitular (diocesan administrator) is elected he is given the bishop's key to the secret archives by the priest mentioned in canon 380. If a bishop is notified of his transfer, and continues for a time to govern his diocese (*sedes a qua*) as a vicar capitular (diocesan administrator), he would retain his key until he leaves to take canonical possession of his new diocese (*sedes ad quam*). Upon his departure the priest mentioned in canon 380 would assume the bishop's key until a new bishop, a vicar capitular (diocesan administrator) or an apostolic administrator assumes the government of the diocese.

---

[25] Can. 427.

[26] *Ius Canonicum,* II, p. 821, n. 648, footnote 45.

[27] Can. 430, § 1.

[28] Canons 431, § 1, and 432, § 1.

When a diocese becomes vacant, the jurisdiction of the vicar-general ceases. This is true even then when the bishop is transferred to another see but temporarily continues on in the diocese (*sedes a qua*) as vicar capitular (diocesan administrator). Therefore the vicar-general should submit his key to the ranking dignitary of the cathedral chapter or to the oldest diocesan consultor. If at the time of the vacancy of the diocese the chancellor would be in possession of the second key by virtue of the ruling contained in canon 379, § 3, he should surrender the key to the ranking dignitary of the cathedral chapter or to the oldest diocesan consultor.

Article II. Sealing of the Archives

Can. 381, § 2: "Antequam claves iis, quibus tradi debent ad normam § 1, remissae fuerint, Vicarius Generalis vel cancellarius et sacerdos, ut supra, ab Episcopo designatus, tabularium vel armarium sigillis Curiae obsignent."

As an additional precaution in the custody of the material in the secret archives when the see is impeded or vacant, the law requires the sealing of the archives. This must be done by the two persons legitimately in possession of the keys before the keys are transferred to the new authorized persons. Therefore either the vicar-general or the chancellor and the priest designated according to canon 380 are obliged to seal the archives when the see becomes impeded or vacant.

Whether the sealing should be done only if a vicar capitular (or diocesan administrator) assumes the administration of the diocese is not certain. Blat,[29] Mathias[30] and others believe that the sealing of the archives is required only if a vicar capitular (or diocesan administrator) is chosen. The fact that only in such a circumstance are both keys involved in a transfer seems to be the basis for their argument. But, actually, the ecclesiastic who is elected vicar capitular (or diocesan administrator) may easily have been the vicar-general (chancellor) or the priest designated according to canon 380. The vicar capitular (or diocesan administrator) would, therefore, again be entitled to possess one of the keys, and only one of the keys would change hands.

Louis is probably more correct when he maintains that "it is undoubtedly the mind of the legislator to provide for this special protection of sealing the

---

[29] *Commentarium*, II, p. 411, nn. 417-418.

[30] *Diocesan Curia*, p. 282.

secret archives whenever the see is impeded or vacant, without reference to the person upon whom the administration of the diocese devolves in the circumstances under consideration."[31] The law does not distinguish, and the purpose of the law seems to be better served if no distinction is invoked. Therefore the sealing of the archives should be observed whenever there is an interregnum between residential bishops.

The appointment of a permanent apostolic administrator is the appointment of a person having all the rights of a residential bishop, and therefore this seems to provide the only possible exception to canon 381, § 2. *De facto,* indeed, the permanent apostolic administrator is not mentioned or contemplated in either paragraph of canon 381. But since he has all the rights of a residential bishop, and since the right of ready access to the secret archives is not excluded, the secret archives should not be sealed when he assumes the government of the diocese.

What the actual sealing should consist in is not stated. Most likely a sufficient method would obtain through the sealing of the entrance in such a way that any opening of the entrance will break the seal. This may be accomplished with the use of wire and lead and sealing wax of some kind impressed with the diocesan seal. No matter what method is used, the two persons responsible for the sealing must conscientiously fulfill this obligation as soon as possible.

Therefore, by means of two keys and the sealing of the archives the Church seeks to protect the secret archives from all tampering or unlawful entry. The legislation of the Code is sufficiently precise to ensure adequate custody of the contents of the secret archives.

---

[31] *Diocesan Archives,* p. 81.

CHAPTER VI. USE OF THE SECRET ARCHIVES

In the administration of his diocese, the bishop may obtain documents which are of a secret character either by their very nature or by a determination of the law. It is his responsibility to use and perhaps preserve these secret documents according to law. When he commits these documents to the diocesan secret archives, he does not hamper his access to them but simply guarantees their safe depository. The security of such documents is particularly important whenever the see is vacant or quasi-vacant. Therefore, there are enacted in the Code definite regulations whereby the secret archives may be protected from unauthorized use, both when the bishop is governing his diocese and when the see is vacant or impeded.

Article I. When the See is Occupied

Can. 379, § 4: *Episcopus vel Administrator Apostolicus, repetita altera clave, ipse solus, nemine adstante, archivum vel armarium secretum, ubi opus fuerit, aperire et inspicere potest, quod deinde utraque clavi iterum claudatur.*

The canon explicitly reserves to the bishop of the diocese the right to use the secret archives. The apostolic administrator mentioned in canon 379, § 4, is undoubtedly one who has been permanently appointed to administer a diocese. A permanently appointed apostolic administrator has all the rights and duties of a residential bishop.[1] For that reason he is mentioned in canon 379, § 4, as having the same right to use the secret archives. Either one of these two enjoys the fullness of the rights of a residential bishop. And therefore either one of these two may, when necessary for whatever reason, open and inspect the secret archives without any witnesses.[2] All other persons, of whatever rank, are excluded.[3]

An apostolic administrator appointed for a limited time has all the rights and duties of a vicar capitular.[4] Therefore in using the secret archives he

[1] Can. 315, § 1.

[2] Ayrinhac, *Constitution of the Church,* p. 220; Coronata, I-II, p. 508, footnote n. 4.

[3] Jone, *Commentarium in Codicem Iuris Canonici,* I (Paderborn: Schöningh, 1950), p. 305 (hereafter cited as *Commentarium.*)

[4] Can. 315, § 2, n. 1.

would follow the norms established for vicars capitular. These norms will be considered in detail subsequently.

In order to use this right of access to the secret archives, the bishop or the apostolic administrator must claim the other key to the archives from the vicar-general or the chancellor. The "*repetita altera clave*" of the canon clearly indicates the right to demand the second key. Inasmuch as the bishop always has the right of entrance to the archives, the vicar-general or the chancellor cannot refuse to surrender the second key. His custody of the key serves the exclusive purpose of preventing an unauthorized entrance to the archives, but the bishop's entrance is always permitted. A vicar-general or a chancellor who would refuse to surrender his key to the bishop would be violating the bishop's rightful authority over the archives and, in fact, would be usurping the latter's authority over the secret archives.

The only restrictions placed on the bishop by the Code are the conditions that there be some necessity for opening and inspecting the archives, and that the archives be locked with both keys when he is finished. The necessity spoken of in the canon need not be grave; any legitimate necessity would suffice, even his anxiety to guarantee that everything is in order. The importance of relocking the archives with both keys is evident; the strict intent of the law in its precise determinations concerning the custody of the keys would be rendered null if the principal custodian failed to protect the archives by diligently fulfilling all the prescriptions of the law.

Although the law makes no mention of a delegate either of the bishop or of the apostolic administrator, it seems evident that for a good reason a delegate could be permitted access to the secret archives. Jone does not think that it is forbidden to the bishop to allow the vicar-general or the chancellor to enter and inspect the archives, especially to draw up or to complete the *inventarium*.[5] The vicar-general or the chancellor would be the most logical person to serve as a delegate, but surely the bishop is not restricted to these two. The nature of the documents to be studied, or his special confidence in a certain priest, could be a sufficient reason in warrant of the bishop's choice of a priest other than the vicar-general or the chancellor.

In permitting someone to open the archives and to examine the secret documents, the bishop may or may not impose conditions. For example, in per-

---

[5] *Commentarium*, I, 305.

mitting the chancellor to draw up or to complete the *inventarium* the bishop may insist that one of the vice-chancellors be present as a witness as long as the chancellor performs this function. Or in permitting the vicar-general to examine the documents the bishop may demand that the granting of this permission be never mentioned to anyone. As the principal custodian of the secret archives he bears full responsibility for the preservation and use of these secret documents. And since the law explicitly states that he (or the apostolic administrator) alone may without witnesses enter and examine these documents, he should closely adhere to this prescript unless he has good reason to disregard it.

The law in canon 379 makes no mention regarding the removal of any documents from the secret archives. Later, in canon 382, § 1, the vicar capitular is forbidden to remove any documents. Coronata believes that, inasmuch as such a prohibition is not expressed in reference to the bishop or the apostolic administrator, the prohibition does not extend to them.[6] Other authors are not so explicit on the question. Most of them merely state in general that no documents may ever be taken from the secret archives.[7] As a general principle, this is true. But even the law demands that certain documents be burned after a determined period of time, as was seen earlier. The law also demands that certain information in the secret archives, once it has ceased to remain secret, be transferred to public registers or archives. Furthermore, the bishop is free to use the secret archives for any confidential materials according to his discretion, and to remove them later. It seems evident, therefore, that Coronata's opinion is more in harmony not only with the text of the law but also with the purpose of the law in establishing secret archives for the bishop's use in administering his diocese.

Article II. When the See is Impeded or Vacant

Can. 382, § 1: *Tabularium vel armarium nunquam aperiatur nec sigilla ab eo removeantur, nisi urgente necessitate et ab ipso Vicario Capitulari coram duobus canonicis vel dioecesanis consultoribus, qui evigilent ne qua scriptura e tabulario auferatur; solus autem Vicarius Capitularis documenta in tabulario*

---

[6] *Institutiones*, I-II, p. 509, footnote n. 2.

[7] E. g., Prümmer, *Manuale Iuris Canonici* (3. ed., Friburgi: Herder & Co., 1922), Q. 134, n. 4; Coochi, *Commentarium in Codicem Iuris Canonici*, Vol. III (4 ed., Taurinorum Augustae: Marietti, 1940), p. 276; Sipos, p. 263.

asservata potest, iisdem canonicis vel consultoribus adstantibus, inspicere nunquam tamen auferre. Archivum autem, post inspectionem, iterum sigillis obsignetur.

§ 2: *Advenienti novo Episcopo, si sigilla remota fuerint et tabularium aut armarium apertum, Vicarius Capitularis rationem reddat urgentis necessitatis, qua ad hoc motus fuerit.*

The safety and security of the secret archives when the diocese is vacant or quasi-vacant is of especial concern to the legislator because of the danger of abuse when the usual supervision is apt to be relaxed. The prescript to seal the archives whenever there is an interregnum between residential bishops has already been treated. The question here concerns two distinct acts: the breaking of this seal and the opening of the archives. Canon 382, § 1, determines the conditions under which the secret archives may be used when the diocese is vacant or quasi-vacant.

The first condition postulated in the law is that an urgent necessity be present. Louis cites three examples of urgent necessity: to inscribe in their proper books records recently received concerning a marriage of conscience, or regarding a dispensation granted in the internal non-sacramental forum, or to study the acts of a current criminal process which are already in the archives.[8]

The second condition determines who may use the secret archives when the see is vacant or quasi-vacant. The two distinct acts of breaking the seal and of opening the archives are specifically reserved to the vicar capitular (or diocesan administrator). Since an apostolic administrator who is temporarily appointed to the see has a status equivalent to that of a vicar capitular, he would be included under the same norms enacted for the vicar capitular.

As stated earlier in Article II of the previous Chapter, the sealing of the archives is to take place whenever the see is impeded or vacant. And therefore, if the see is impeded and the vicar-general or a priest delegated by the bishop is administering the diocese, the secret archives must be sealed. And if the secret archives must be used during such an administration, the vicar-general or the priest delegated by the bishop would follow the norms enacted in canon 382, § 1, for the vicar capitular.

---

[8] *Diocesan Archives*, p. 84.

In reserving the use of the secret archives to the vicar capitular (or diocesan administrator), the law invokes a further limitation. He may break the seal and open the archives only in the presence of two canons or diocesan consultors. This is stated in contradistinction to what is not required of the bishop or the apostolic administrator, who may inspect the archives without witnesses, as was seen in the previous Article. Therefore, a vicar capitular or a diocesan administrator may never disregard this statute; he may never inspect the secret archives without the two witnesses required by law. Since the law does not specify which canons or diocesan consultors should be chosen as witnesses, Louis rightly concludes that the vicar, capitular or the diocesan administrator may choose any two whom he wishes.[9] The law imposes on them simply the obligation of vigilance, so that none of the documents will be removed. There is not given to them the right to inspect the archives or the documents.

A further determination in the law leaves no doubt regarding the one who may examine the documents. Once he has broken the seal and opened the archives, the vicar capitular (or diocesan administrator) alone may inspect the documents, although the two canons or consultors stand by to fulfill their obligation. Coronata believes that the vicar capitular (or diocesan administrator) can, if there is a need, delegate someone to inspect the documents for him, as long as the latter observes the same conditions which the law postulates for the vicar capitular in his use of the archives.[10] Louis agrees with this opinion, for he maintains that the vicar capitular (or diocesan administrator) has the ordinary jurisdiction of a bishop in all spiritual and temporal affairs except in those which are expressly prohibited to him by law, and the Code does not expressly forbid him to grant this permission.[11]

Having conceded to the vicar capitular (diocesan administrator) the right to examine the documents in the secret archives, the canon immediately forbids him to remove any of the documents. This prohibition stands contrary to the previous enactments in the law which require that certain documents be removed and burned, or transferred to public registers or archives. But the prohibition stands, and may not be disregarded by the vicar capitular (diocesan administrator). The removal of any documents for whatever reason,

---

[9] *Diocesan Archives*, p. 85.

[10] *Institutiones*, I, p. 509, footnote n. 3.

[11] *Diocesan Archives*, pp. 85-86.

howsoever legitimate, must await the arrival of a permanent apostolic administrator or a new residential bishop.

Finally, upon satisfying the need of consulting the secret archives, the vicar capitular (diocesan administrator) is responsible for the closing and the sealing of the archives. He may not postpone this function for any length of time, lest the purpose of the law be nullified. In closing the archives he must employ both locks and thereupon return the second key to the person designated by law. When sealing the archives, the vicar capitular (diocesan administrator) may use either the same method and materials that were previously used, or some other adequate method of sealing.

In order to safeguard the secret archives from even the slightest misuse, the law sets an additional requirement. If the vicar capitular (diocesan administrator) has found it necessary to make use of his prerogative to examine certain documents in the secret archives, the law demands that he explain to the new residential bishop the reasons that prompted him at the time. In this way the law seeks to prevent mere whim or curiosity from dictating any unnecessary use of the secret archives. And while the law places this obligation specifically on the vicar capitular (diocesan administrator), the same obligation seems to apply to a vicar-general or a priest delegated by the bishop to administer the diocese when the bishop is impeded, or to an apostolic administrator who has only a temporary appointment to the see. It has already been shown that all of these individuals have a status equivalent to that of a vicar capitular, and therefore must observe all the obligations imposed on a vicar capitular.

The Code is exact and definite in the regulations governing the use of the secret archives. Whether a diocese be vacant or quasi-vacant, there are, in relation to documents in the secret archives, precise rules and conditions that govern the responsibility of the person administering the diocese. When the documents must be used, whoever is responsible for the regimen of the diocese is able to determine what is permitted to him and how he must thereby fulfill his office.

CHAPTER VII. PENALTIES FOR VIOLATIONS INFRINGING ON THE SECRET ARCHIVES

Although there are no sanctions wherewith the Code specifically punishes violations infringing on the diocesan secret archives, several penal sanctions as pertaining to the abuse of an office or the misuse of documents are applicable. These penalties the lawgiver has enacted in order to help safeguard the ecclesiastical system of legal proof through authentic documents.[1] The canons in question are:

All those who forge or falsify letters or acts of an ecclesiastical character or pertaining to ecclesiastical matters, whether public or private, and all who knowingly use the same forged or falsified documents, are to be penalized according to the gravity of the delinquency.[2]

Anyone who, having been appointed officially to catalogue, write or preserve such books or documents, presumes to falsify, adulterate, destroy, or conceal them, is to be deprived of his office and otherwise severely punished by the ordinary according to the gravity of the fault.[3]

The abuse of ecclesiastical authority shall be punished at the discretion of the legitimate superior in proportion to the gravity of the guilt, without prejudice to the specific penalties enacted in the Code for certain abuses.[4]

Persons who are in charge of the records or books and who maliciously refuse when legitimately requested to transcribe, transmit, or exhibit the acts, documents or books, or who in any other way abuse their office, may be punished with deprivation of or suspension from office, and with fines at the discretion of the ordinary and in proportion to the gravity of guilt in the various cases.[5]

Persons who increase or exact more than the customary taxes, legitimately approved in accordance with canon 1507, shall be restrained by a heavy mone-

---

[1] Prince, p. 88.
[2] Can. 2362.
[3] Can. 2406, § 1.
[4] Can. 2404.
[5] Can. 2406, § 2.

tary fine, and, if they fail again, shall be suspended or removed from office in proportion to the gravity of their guilt, without prejudice to their obligation of making restitution of the money unjustly acquired.[6]

These penalties are all vindicative, which means that they have for their primary object the good of the community, the expiation of the crime, and the restoration of a violated social order. Unlike censures, they look primarily to the delict committed, that is, to the violation of the law, rather than to the offender or violator of the law. Hence the amendment of the delinquent does not give him the right to be released from these penalties, as is true of censures, and, furthermore, these penalties are inflicted for a definite time or *in perpetuum.*[7]

Vindicative penalties can be either *latae sententiae* or *ferendae sententiae* punishments. The penalties here considered are all of a *ferendae sententiae* character, which means that they are to be inflicted by the judge or a superior.

It may likewise be noted that the vindicative penalties under consideration are all undetermined or facultative. In other words, the specification of what the penalties are to be is left to the prudent discretion of the judge or superior. At times his discretion may relate even to the question whether any penalty at all is to be inflicted, as well as to question of the kind of penalty, or the measure in which, or the length of time for which, it is to be imposed.

The remission of vindicative penalties is generally effected by means of a dispensation. If they were inflicted for a definite time or under a certain condition, they cease of themselves when the time has elapsed or the condition is fulfilled.[8]

Article I. In Reference to the Residential Bishop

As the principal custodian of the diocesan secret archives, the bishop would have to answer with the primary responsibility if these archives were misused

---

[6] Can. 2408.

[7] Cf. Ayrinhac-Lydon, *Penal Legislation in the New Code of Canon Law* (rev. ed., New York: Benziger Brothers, 1936), p. 116, n. 156; also Vermeersch-Creusen, *Epitome Iuris Canonici,* Vol. III (6. ed., Mechliniae: Dessain, 1946), p. 294, n. 489 (hereafter cited as Vermeersch-Creusen).

[8] Christ, *Dispensation from Vindicative Penalties,* The Catholic University of America Canon Law Studies, n. 174 (Washington, D. C.: The Catholic University of America Press, 1943), pp. 65 ff.

or violated in any way. But in the event of a violation, it must be ascertained whether the residential bishop is guilty of a delict as delineated in the penal legislation of the Code, and what must be done about the matter.

The Code provides that residential bishops can be judged by the Sovereign Pontiff alone,[9] and can be punished only by him, whether by way of condemnatory or by way of declaratory sentence.[10]

Therefore, if a residential bishop has been guilty of any of the above-mentioned delicts, he can be punished by the Sovereign Pontiff alone. As already seen, the involved *ferendae sententiae* penalties are undetermined, and therefore it depends on the discretion of the Sovereign Pontiff whether any penalty is to be inflicted and what is to be the kind of penalty and its measure. And, furthermore, the remission of these penalties will be reserved to the Sovereign Pontiff or to whomever he has committed this power.[11]

Since the diocesan secret archives are expressly committed to the local ordinary as a means of facilitating and assisting his administration of the diocese, he is presumed to be a worthy administrator. Therefore, any complaints or accusations against his administration must be taken to the authority who constituted him in office. Furthermore, the use of the secret archives rests with the local ordinary so that, if he decides that a document may not be made public, or if made public that it may not bear all the names involved, this decision may, far from being an abuse of his office, reflect rather his prudent judgment in the case. And therefore, unless his violation or the abuse in such matters is patently flagrant, it would be foolhardy to question his authority or responsibility, and very difficult to prove the existence of *dolus,* i. e., the *deliberata voluntas violandi legem.*[12]

The same may be said of a possible violation of canon 2408. Thus, only if the residential bishop were to demand an exorbitant tax for a rescript from the diocesan secret archives, could one begin to think of recourse to the Holy See. The residential bishop is presumed to have a sufficient reason to justify his action.

---

[9] Can. 1557, § 1, n. 3.

[10] Can. 2227, § 1.

[11] Can. 2236, § 1.

[12] Can. 2200, § 1.

On the other hand, the constant practice of the Church is to make it possible for all who have serious grievances to be able to seek redress. And therefore, should a grave violation be evident, the victim, whether cleric or lay, may and should take advantage of the right recognized in the common law to approach the proper superiors.

Article II. In Reference to the Vicar Capitular

The responsibility of a vicar capitular (or a diocesan administrator) in regard to the custody and use of the diocesan secret archives while the see is vacant has already been discussed. Canon 382, § 1, permits the vicar capitular (or diocesan administrator) alone to break the seal, to open the archives, and to inspect the contents, but definite restrictions are placed upon him in the same canon, as has been seen.

The vicar capitular is primarily singled out in canon 435, § 3, which forbids the removal, destruction, concealment, or alterations of any curial documents. There is no doubt that canon 382, § 1, and canon 435, § 3, seek to guarantee the security of archival documents during the vacancy of the see. These dispositions of the law become reinforced through the penal sanctions enacted in the canons already cited.

The vicar capitular (or diocesan administrator), therefore, who assumes the regimen of the vacant diocese assumes likewise all the responsibilities and obligations of the office. And one of the grave responsibilities is the custody of the diocesan secret archives. If he is guilty of any of the violations enumerated above, he is to be punished according to law. Since the penal sanctions are all of a *ferendae sententiae* character, and since they are to be inflicted by the superior, it may be noted here that the superior of the vicar capitular during the vacancy of the diocese is the Sovereign Pontiff, but when the diocese has received a new residential bishop, the latter becomes the superior for the inflicting of the needed or called for punishment.[13]

The forging or falsifying of a document can hardly ever be excused. But if, in his capacity as the ordinary, the vicar capitular decides that a document

---

[13] Vermeersch-Creusen, III, p. 383, n. 611.

may not be made public, or that he will conceal a part of the information, the decision pertains to his discretionary power, and he can hardly be punished for prudently administering his power according to his conscience and knowledge. If it can be proved that his administration was incompetent and sinfully mismanaged, then the violation infringing on the secret archives would probably be only a part of the accusations, and the punishment will derive from the total maladministration, and not be an accumulation of all the penalties inflicted for various specific delicts.

If the vicar capitular removes a document or record of the secret archives in violation of canon 382, § 1, and 435, § 3, the removal itself would hardly constitute a grave matter unless some other circumstance existed. Thus, if during the removal a grave harm or inconvenience could readily be foreseen to result because of the removal, or if the removed document could similarly be foreseen to become the cause of grave harm when used by anyone other than the competent superior, the removal would be a serious violation.[14]

If the vicar capitular is guilty of any of the delicts mentioned above, the legitimate superior has the right and the duty to punish him according to the gravity of the guilt. The law provides for a report by the vicar capitular to the new residential bishop, either if the seal of the secret archives was removed, or if the archives were opened. In making this report he should include an explanation for his concealment or change of any records as well as any other transactions envisioned in canon 435, § 3. It should be pointed out that paragraphs 1 and 2 of canon 2406 postulate the perfect *dolus* spoken of in canon 2229, § 2, in regard to these acts of abuse of office. And therefore the new residential bishop cannot indiscriminately punish any concealment, alteration, etc., of secret archive documents, unless it is evident that the vicar capitular acted with grave malice. The vicar capitular is presumed to have acted according to prudent discretion unless the contrary is evident in the case.

Article III. In Reference to Others

The function of the vicar-general in connection with the diocesan secret archives is usually limited to the custody of the second key.[15] It has been noted

[14] Vermeersch-Creusen, III, p. 383, n. 611.

[15] Can. 379, § 3.

that the vicar-general could logically serve as the delegate of the residential bishop in entering and inspecting the secret archives. Ordinarily, however, the vicar-general does not have access to the secret archives, nor has he any responsibility regarding them, except for the custody of the second key.

Nevertheless, it is possible that the penalties under consideration may apply to him. For instance, if he was given access to the secret archives as the bishop's delegate and at the time destroyed, concealed, or otherwise violated the archives, he would be liable to the *ferendae sententiae* penalties. The residential bishop would be the legitimate superior to inflict the penalties according to the norms of law.

The chancellor has even less responsibility in law over the diocesan secret archives than the vicar-general. He would be entrusted with the second key if there were no vicar-general, or if the latter were absent for any length of time. Just as the vicar-general, so also the chancellor, could serve as the delegate of the residential bishop in entering and inspecting the secret archives. As the archivist for the ordinary archives of the diocese, the chancellor would be the logical person to arrange and dispose the documents of the secret archives in a logical and practical setup.

If the chancellor, by way of grave neglect of his delegated duties or through the deliberate abuse of his delegation, would violate the secret archives, the residential bishop should punish him severely.[16]

Other persons susceptible to penalty could be anyone, cleric or lay, when delegated by the residential bishop to handle, deliver, copy or otherwise use documents of the secret archives. If he misuses the power delegated to him, he should be punished according to the gravity of the guilt.[17] This would be true, for instance, of the priest appointed according to canon 380 to assume custody of the episcopal key when the see becomes vacant or quasi-vacant. Or, another situation could involve the priest delegated by the bishop, according to canon 366, § 3, to administer the diocese when it is quasi-vacant and when the vicar-general is absent or impeded. Such positions of trust are contemplated in the law, and a misuse of this power ought to be severely punished.

---

[16] Prince, pp. 86-89.

[17] Can. 2406, § 1.

With the enacted penal sanctions the lawgiver intends to protect the ecclesiastical system of legal proof through authentic documents. Abuses of this legal trust and authority would tend to undermine the legal system whereby highly confidential documents and records are preserved for the good administration of the diocese. Therefore, the responsibility of the residential bishop extends not only to the erection of secret achives, but also to the careful custody and warranted use thereof. For the fulfillment of this responsibility he may have to resort to the inflicting of penalties for the serious violations which on occasion may exist.

CONCLUSIONS

1. No explicit universal legislation requiring diocesan secret archives existed before the promulgation of the Code of Canon Law.

2. The maintenance and the custody of the diocesan secret archives pertain to the executive or administrative function of the local ordinary and are explicit obligations placed on him by the Code.

3. The secret archives, either as a separate room or as a safe in the general archives, must be such as to guarantee complete protection to the contents therein. The normal, prudent protections against burglary, fire and other dangers suffice for the secret archives.

4. Records of the granting of marriage dispensations for occult impediments must be kept in a special register in the secret archives. Loose documents or papers regarding such dispensations are not in accordance with the law. The Code's prescription regarding the burning of certain documents certainly does not apply to these records.

5. The local ordinary is constituted as the sole authority for deciding when and in what manner marriage of conscience records, whether of the marriage or of the child's subsequent baptism, may be issued.

6. The local ordinary should make every effort to keep the secret archives free of materials and documents that have no rightfully warranted existence in this specialized depository.

7. With regard to holy orders, the records of dispensations from occult irregularities and impediments must be kept in the secret archives, not simply for the protection of the good name of the individual, but also in warrant of the lawfulness and the validity of the sacrament. When the record has been transcribed in the special register of the secret archives, the original document must be destroyed. The local ordinary is free to withhold any release of this secret information, as he prudently sees fit.

8. With regard to criminal cases, the prescribed or implied use of the secret archives for such cases illustrates the care and solicitude of the Church

to guard the rights of every individual and yet to maintain an efficient administration of justice.

9. The Code's enactments for the safeguarding of other confidential documents appear to warrant the use of the secret archives likewise for the baptismal records of adopted persons. The chancellor is the logical person to be delegated by the bishop to enter these records in a special register and to issue certificates of them.

10. The requisite essential secrecy for the acts of the ordinary processes of beatification and canonization as well as the *mens legislatoris* seems to postulate more than ordinary care and custody for these acts, and at times to imply the use of the secret archives.

11. The rule of burning the documents of criminal cases regarding bad behavior applies even if no condemnation has been pronounced in the case. When the delinquent dies, all the documents of his case are to be burned, and not even a summary of the case along with the text of the final sentence is to be retained. If the summary and the text of the final sentence have been preserved beyond the ten-year period, they are in turn to be burned when the delinquent dies.

12. The sealing of the archives should be observed whenever there is an interregnum between residential bishops. No matter what method is used, the two persons responsible for the sealing must conscientiously fulfill this obligation as soon as possible.

13. For a good reason the residential bishop may permit someone, especially the vicar general or the chancellor, to have access to the secret archives as his delegate.

BIBLIOGRAPHY

SOURCES

Acta et Decreta Concilii Plenarii Baltimorensis III, A.D. MDCCCLXXXIV, Baltimore: John Murphy, 1886.

Acta et Decreta Sacrorum Conciliorum Recentiorum, Collectio Lacensis, 7 vols., Friburgi Brisgoviae, 1870-1892.

Bullarum Diplomatum et Privilegiorum Romanorum Pontificum Taurinensis Editio, 24 vols. et Appendix, Augustae Taurinorum, 1857-1872.

Codex Iuris Canonici Pii X Pontificis Maximi iussu digestus, Benedicti Papae XV auctoriate promulgatus, Praefatione, Fontium Annotatione et Indice Analytico-Alphabetico ab Emo Petro Card. Gasparri Auctus, Romae, Typis Polyglottis Vaticanis, 1917; reimpressio, 1934.

Codicis Iuris Canonici Fontes, cura Emi Petri Card. Gasparri editi, 9 vols., Romae (postea Civitate Vaticana): Typis Polyglottis Vaticanis, 1923-1939. (Vols. VII-IX, ed. cura et studio Emi Iustiniani Card. Serédi).

Corpus Iuris Canonici, ed. Lipsiensis secunda, post Aemilii Richteri curas. . . . instruxit Aemilius Friedberg, 2 vols., Lipsiae, 1879-1881.

Decretum Gratiani emendatum et notationibus illustratum cum glossis, Gregorii XIII, Pont. Max., iussu editum, 2 vols., Romae, 1582.

Duchesne, Louis. *Le Liber Pontificalis*, 2 vols., Paris, 1886-1892.

Hardouin, Jean, *Acta Conciliorum et Epistolae Decretales ac Constitutiones Summorum Pontificum*, 12 vols., Parisiis, 1714-1715.

Jaffé, Philippus, *Regesta Pontificum Romanorum ab condita Ecclesia ad annum post Christum natum MCXCVIII*, ed. 2 correctam et auctam auspiciis Gulielmi Wattenbach curaverunt S. Loewenfeld, F. Kaltenbrunner, P. Ewald, 2 vols., Lipsiae, 1885-1888.

Lucanae Ecclesiae Synodus Dioecesana, Lucae, 1887.

Mansi, Joannes, *Sacrorum Conciliorum Nova et Amplissima Collectio*, 53 vols. in 60, Parisiis, 1901-1927.

Monumenta Germaniae Historica, Leges, 5 toms., Toms. I, II, III, et IV, ed. Georgius Pertz, Hannoverae, 1835-1868, Tom. V, ed. Societas aperiedis fontibus rerum germanicarum medii aevi, Hannoverae, 1899.

Monumenta Germaniae Historica, Legum Sectio II, Capitularia Regum Francorum, 2 toms., edd. Alfredus Boretius et Victor Krause, Hannoverae, Tom. I, 1890; Tom. II, 1897.

Monumenta Germaniae Historica, Legum Sectio III, Concilia aevi merovingici, Tom. I, ed. Fredericus Maassen, Hannoverae, 1893.

Quaranta, Stephanus, *Summa Bullarii Earumve Summorum Pontificum Constitutionum*, Venetiis, 1622.

Ratti, Achille (later Pope Pius XI), *Acta Ecclesiae Mediolanensis ab ejus Initiis usque ad Nostram Aetatem*, 3 vols., Mediolani, 1890-1892.

Rozière, Eugène de, *Liber Diurnus*, Paris, 1869.

Thesaurus Resolutionum Sacrae Congregationis Concilii, 167 vols., Urbini, 1718-1741; Romae, 1741-1908.

REFERENCE WORKS

Abbo, John—Hannan, Jerome, *The Sacred Canons*, 2 vols., St. Louis: B. Herder Book Co., 1952.

Augustine, Charles, *A Commentary on the New Code of Canon Law*, 8 vols., Vol. II, 3. ed., St. Louis: Herder, 1919; Vol. IV, 2. ed., St. Louis: Herder, 1923.

Ayrinhac, H. A., *Constitution of the Church*, New York: Longmans, Green and Co., 1929.

Ayrinhac, H. A.—Lydon, P. J., *Marriage Legislation in the New Code of Canon Law*. rev. ed., New York: Benziger Brothers, 1949.

——————, *Penal Legislation in the New Code of Canon Law*, rev. ed., New York: Benziger Brothers, 1936.

Barraclough, Geoffrey, *Papal Provisions*, Oxford; Basil Blackwell, 1935.

Beste, Udalricus, *Introductio in Codicem*, 3 ed., Collegeville, Minn.: St. John's Abbey Press, 1946.

Bingham, Joseph, *The Antiquities of the Christian Church*, 2 vols., London, 1856.

Blaher, Damian, *The Ordinary Process in Causes of Beatification and Canonization*, The Catholic University of America Canon Law Studies, n. 268, Washington, D. C.: The Catholic Univerisity of America Press, 1949.

Blat, Albertus, *Commentarium Textus Iuris Canonici*, 6 vols., Vol. II, Lib. II, 2. ed.. Romae, 1921.

Bouard, A., *Manuel de diplomatique francaise et pontificale*, Paris, 1929.

Bouix, D., *Tractatus de Judiciis Ecclesiasticis*, 2 vols., Parisiis, 1855.

Bouscaren, T. Lincoln—Ellis, Adam, *Canon Law*, 2. rev. ed., Milwaukee: The Bruce Publishing Co., 1951.

Bresslau, Harry, *Handbuch der Urkundenlehre für Deutschland und Italien*, 2 ed., 2. vols., Leipzig, 1912.

Brunini, Joseph, *The Clerical Obligations of Canons 139 and 142*, The Catholic University of America Canon Law Studies, n. 103, Washington, D. C.: The Catholic University of America, 1937.

Campagna, Angelo, *Il Vicario Generale del Vescovo*, The Catholic University of America Canon Law Studies, n. 66, Washington, D. C.: The Catholic University of America, 1921.

Cappello, F., *Summa Iuris Canonici*, 3 vols., Vol. II, 4. ed., Romae: Apud Aedes Universitatis Gregorianae, 1945.

——————, *Tractatus Canonico-Moralis de Sacramentis*, 5 vols., Vol. V, 6. ed., Taurini-Romae, 1950.

Casey, James, *A Study of Canon 2222*, § 1, The Catholic University of America Canon Law Studies, n. 290, Washington, D. C.: The Catholic University of America Press, 1949.

Cerchiari, E., *Cappellani Papae et Apostolicae Sedis, Auditores Causarum Sacri Palatii Apostolici seu S. R. Rotae, ab Origine ad Diem usque 20 sept. 1870*, 4 vols., Romae, 1919-1921.

Chelodi, I, *Ius Poenale*, Tridenti: Libr. Edit. Tridentum, 1925 [1920?].

Chelodi, I.—Ciprotti, P., *Ius Canonicum de Matrimonio*, 5. ed., Vicenza: Societa Anonima, Tipografica Editrice, 1947.

Cicognani, Amleto, *Canon Law,* 2 ed., Reprint, Westminster, Md.: The Newman Press, 1949.

Coburn, Vincent, *Marriages of Conscience,* The Çatholic University of America. Canon Law Studies, n. 191, Washington, D. C.: The Catholic University of America Press, 1944.

Cocchi, Guidus, *Commentarium in Codicem Iuris Canonici,* 8 vols. in 5, Vol. III, 4. ed., Taurinorum Augustae: Marietti, 1940.

Concilium Romanum, 1725. Romae: ex Typographia Rocchi Bernabò, 1725.

Connolly, Thomas, *Appeals,* The Catholic University of America Canon Law Studies, n. 79, Washington, D. C.: The Catholic University of America, 1932.

Coronata, Matthaeus Conte a, *Institutiones Iuris Canonici,* 5 vols., Vols. I-II, 4. ed., Taurini: Marietti, 1950-1951.

——————, *Manuale Practicum Iuris Disciplinaris et Criminalis Regularium,* Romae: Marietti, 1938.

D'Angelo, Sosio, *La Curia Diocesana, a norma del Codice di Diritto Canonico,* Giarre (Sicilia): Pietro Lisi, 1922.

De Lugo. *Disputationes de iustitia et de iure,* 2 ed., 2 vols., Venetiis, 1718.

Doheny, W., *Canonical Procedure in Matrimonial Cases,* 2 vols., Vol. I, *Formal Judicial Procedure,* 2 ed., Milwaukee: Bruce Publishing Co.. 1947.

Dougherty, John, *De Inquisitione Speciali,* The Catholic University of America Canon Law Studies, n. 213, Washington, D. C.: The Catholic University of America Press, 1945.

Duerr, Charles, *The Judicial Notary,* The Catholic University of America Canon Law Studies, n. 312, Washington, D. C.: The Catholic University of America Press, 1951.

Eagleton, George, *The Diocesan Quinquennial Faculties, Formula IV,* The Catholic University of America Canon Law Studies, n. 248, Washington, D. C.: The Catholic University of America Press, 1948.

Esswein, Anthony, *Extrajudicial Coercive Powers of Ecclesiastical Superiors,* The Catholic University of America Canon Law Studies, n. 127, Washington, D. C.: The Catholic University of America Press, 1941.

Fagnanus, Prosper, *Commentarium in decretalium libros,* 5 vols., Venetiis, 1709.

Gougnard, Armand, *Tractatus de Matrimonio,* 7 ed., Mechliniae: Dessain, 1931.

Hefele, C. J., *A History of the Councils of the Church,* translated from the German and edited by William H. Clark, Vol. I, Edinburgh, 1883 (2. ed., revised).

Jenkinson, Hilary, *A Manual of Archive Administration,* Oxford: The Clarendon Press, 1922.

Jolowicz, H. F., *Historical Introduction to the Study of Roman Law,* 2. ed., Cambridge: At the University Press, 1952.

Jone, Heribertus, *Commentarium in Codicem Iuris Canonici,* 2 vols., Vol. I, Paderborn: Schöningh, 1950.

Kubelbeck, William, *The Sacred Penitentiaria and its Relation to Faculties of Ordinaries and Priests,* The Catholic University of America Canon Law Studies, n. 5, Washington, D. C.: The Catholic University of America, 1918.

Kurtscheid, Bertrandus, *Historia Iuris Canonici, Historia Institutorum,* Vol. I (ab Ecclesiae fundatione usque ad Gratianum), Romae: Officium Libri Catholici, 1941.

Leage, R. W., *Roman Private Law,* 2 ed., by C. H. Ziegler, London: Macmillan & Co., 1930, reprinted 1946.

Lega, M., *De Iudiciis Ecclesiasticis,* 4 vols., Romae: Typis Vaticanis, 1896-1901.

Lega, M.—Bartoccetti, V., *Commentarius in Iudicia Ecclesiastica iuxta Codicem Iuris Canonici,* 3 vols. and Appendix volume, Romae: Anonima Libreria Cattolica Italiana, 1950.

Louis, William, *Diocesan Archives,* The Catholic University of America Canon Law Studies, n. 137, Washington, D. C.: The Catholic University of America Press, 1941.

Lucidi, Angelus, *De Visitatione Sacrorum Liminum,* 3. ed., 3 vols., Romae, 1883.

Mathias. L., *The Diocesan Curia,* Madras: The Good Pastor Press, 1947.

McDonough, Thomas, *Apostolic Administrators,* The Catholic University of America Canon Law Studies, n. 139, Washington, D. C.: The Catholic University of America Press, 1941.

Meier, Carl, *Penal Administrative Procedure against Negligent Pastors,* The Catholic University of America Canon Law Studies, n. 140, Washington, D. C.: The Catholic University of America Press. 1941.

Migne, Jacques, *Patrologiae Cursus Completus, Series Latina,* 221 vols., Parisiis, 1844-1855.

Monin, A., *De Curia Romana,* Louvain, 1912.

Muirhead, J., *Historical Introduction to the Private Law of Rome,* 3. ed. revised and edited by Alexander Grant, London: A. & C. Black, Ltd., 1916.

Murphy, Edwin, *Suspension ex Informata Conscientia,* The Catholic University of America Canon Law Studies, n. 76, Washington, D. C.: The Catholic University of America, 1932.

O'Rourke, James, *Parish Registers,* The Catholic University of America Canon Law Studies, n. 88, Washington, D. C.: The Catholic University of America, 1934.

Pelliccia, A., *De Politia Christianae Ecclesiae* (ed. J. I. Ritter), Coloniae ad Rhenum, 1829.

Poole, Reginald, *Lectures on the History of the Papal Chancery,* Cambridge: Cambridge Press, 1915.

Popek, Alphonse, *The Rights and Obligations of Metropolitans,* The Catholic University of America Canon Law Studies, n 260, Washington, D. C.: The Catholic University of America Press, 1947.

Prince, John, *The Diocesan Chancellor,* The Catholic University of America Canon Law Studies, n. 167, Washington, D. C.: The Catholic University of America Press, 1942.

Prümmer, Dominicus, *Manuale Iuris Canonici,* 3. ed., Friburgi: Herder & Co., 1922.

Rainer, Eligius, *Suspension of Clerics,* The Catholic University of America Canon Law Studies, n. 111, Washington, D. C.: The Catholic University of America, 1937.

Ramstein, Matthew, *A Manual of Canon Law,* 2. ed. rev., Hoboken, N. J.: Terminal Printing & Publishing Co., 1948.

Ryan, Gerald, *Principles of Episcopal Jurisdiction,* The Catholic University of America Canon Law Studies, n. 120, Washington, D. C.: The Catholic University of America Press, 1939.

Schroeder, H. J., *Disciplinary Decrees of the General Councils,* St. Louis: B. Herder Book Co., 1937.

__________, *Canons and Decrees of the Council of Trent,* St. Louis: B. Herder Book Co., 1941.

Sipos, Stephanus, *Enchiridion Iuris Canonici,* Pécs: Ex Typographia "Haladas R. T.," 1926.

Toso, A., *Ad Codicem Iuris Canonici Commentaria Minora,* 5 vols. in 2, Liber II, *De Personis,* Tom. I, Taurini-Romae, 1922.

Vaughan, William, *Constitutions for Diocesan Courts,* The Catholic University of America Canon Law Studies, n. 210, Washington, D. C.: The Catholic University of America Press, 1944.

Vives y Tuto, Josephus Card., *De Dignitate et Officiis Episcoporum et Praelatorum,* Romae: Pustet, 1905.

Wernz, F.—Vidal, P., *Ius Canonicum ad Codicis Normam Exactum,* 7 vols. in 8, (Vol. II, 3. ed., a P. Aguirre, 1943), Romae: Apud Aedes Universitatis Gregorianae, 1943.

Wolff, H. J., *Roman Law,* Norman, Oklahoma: University of Oklahoma Press, 1951.

ARTICLES

Arthur, E. Robert, "Baptismal Certificates for Adopted Children," *The Jurist,* XIII (1953), 57-79.

Vermeersch, Arthurus, "De Constitutione Vicarii Generalis vel Delegati facta ab Administratore Apostolico," *Periodica,* XIII (1924), 15-17.

BIOGRAPHICAL NOTE

Charles Alvin Kekumano was born on May 12, 1919, at Napoopoo, Kealakekua Bay, Hawaii. He received his primary and high school education at St. Louis College, Honolulu. He spent four years at St. Anthony's Seminary, Santa Barbara, California. Then he entered San Luis Rey Seminary, Oceanside, California, where he completed his philosophical course and received the degree of Bachelor of Arts in 1944. After three years of his theological studies at the Old Mission, Santa Barbara, California, he transferred to St. Patrick's Seminary, Menlo Park, California. He was ordained to the priesthood in Our Lady Queen of Peace Cathedral, Honolulu, on May 26, 1949, by His Excellency, the Most Reverend James J. Sweeney, D.D., Bishop of Honolulu. After a year and a half of parochial work he was assigned to the Chancery in Honolulu for six months, and then was admitted to the School of Canon Law of the Catholic University of America. He received the degree of the Baccalaureate in Canon Law in June, 1952, and the degree of the Licentiate in Canon Law in June, 1953.

CANON LAW STUDIES *

349. Bottoms, Rev. Archibald M., J.C.L., The discretionary authority of the ecclesiastical judge in matrimonial trials of the first instance.

350. Kekumano, Rev. Charles A., A.B., J.C.L., The secret archives of the diocesan curia.

351. McGrath, Rev. Robert Eamon, O.M.I., J.C.L., The local superior in non-exempt clerical congregations.

352. McManus, Rev. Frederick Richard, A.B., J.C.L., The Congregation of Sacred Rites.

353. Rodimer, Rev. Frank J., A.B., S.T.L., J.C.L., The canonical effects of infamy of fact.

354. Rouillard, Rev. Jacques, A.B., Ph. B., J.C.L., Une étude comparée du droit canonique et du droit civil paroissal de la Province de Québec dans l'administration des biens paroissaux.

355. Ryan, Rev. Thomas C., J.C.L., The juridical effects of the *sanatio in radice*.

356. Sullivan, Rev. Bernard Owens, J.C.L., Legislation and requirements for permissible cohabitation in invalid marriages.

357. Tatarczuk, Rev. Vincent Anthony, A.B., S.T.L., J.C.L., Infamy of law.

* For a complete list of the available numbers of this series apply to the Catholic University of America Press, 620 Michigan Ave., N. E., Washington (17), D. C., for a general catalogue.

INDEX

www.ingramcontent.com/pod-product-compliance
Lightning Source LLC
LaVergne TN
LVHW050158080826
844660LV00012B/314
* 9 7 8 0 8 1 3 2 2 5 1 8 0 *